DK EYEWITNESS TRAVEL

TOP 10
CHICAGO

ELAINE GLUSAC
ELISA KRONISH
ROBERTA SOTONOFF

D1020380

FEB   2018

DK | Penguin
Random
House

Top 10 Chicago Highlights

Welcome to Chicago **5**
Exploring Chicago **6**
Chicago Highlights **10**
Willis Tower and Its Views **12**
The Art Institute of Chicago **14**
Field Museum **18**
Museum of Science
    and Industry **20**
Navy Pier **24**
John G. Shedd Aquarium **28**
Lincoln Park Zoo **30**
Magnificent Mile **32**
Millennium Park **34**
Frank Lloyd Wright's Oak Park ...**36**

The Top 10 of Everything

Moments in Chicago History **40**
Skyscrapers **42**
Niche Museums **44**
Parks and Beaches **46**
Film Locations **48**
Off the Beaten Path **50**
Kids' Chicago **52**
Performing Arts **54**
Blues and Jazz Joints **56**
Bars and Clubs **58**
Places to Eat **60**
Shopping Destinations **62**
Chicago for Free **64**
Festivals and Events **66**

CONTENTS

Chicago Area by Area

The Loop.................................**70**
Near North.............................**78**
Northside................................**86**
South Loop.............................**94**
Far South................................**100**

Streetsmart

Getting To and Around
    Chicago **108**
Practical Information................**110**
Places To Stay **116**

General Index..........................**120**
Acknowledgments...................**126**

Within each Top 10 list in this book, no hierarchy of quality or popularity is implied. All 10 are, in the editor's opinion, of roughly equal merit.

Throughout this book, floors are referred to in accordance with American usage; i.e. the "first floor" is at ground level.

***Front cover and spine** Tour boat in downtown Chicago near Michigan Avenue Bridge*
***Back cover** The Neo-Classical building housing the Museum of Science and Industry*
***Title page** The iconic clock outside Macy's and the Chicago Theatre behind on N. State Street*

Welcome to
Chicago

Chicago has been called the "City of the Big Shoulders" for its industrial brawn, the "Second City" for its size, and the "Windy City" for its politics – all of which the city embraces with good-humored warmth, confidence, and imagination. With Eyewitness Top 10 Chicago, it's yours to explore.

The city's own motto is "urbs in horto," or city in a garden, and its connection to nature is readily apparent, from the vast Lake Michigan shoreline to the Chicago River that divides the city. Its public living room is art-filled **Millennium Park**, and its playground is **Navy Pier**, jutting into the lake with carnival-like attractions as well as more high-minded distractions such as the Chicago Shakespeare Theater. Both the **Lincoln Park Zoo** and the **John G. Shedd Aquarium** offer exposure to natural life beyond the region.

Culture abounds indoors and out. Birthplace of the skyscraper, Chicago has a range of architecture spanning the lofty **Willis Tower** and the earth-grounded Prairie School homes of Frank Lloyd Wright in **Oak Park**. Museums are similarly diverse, from the **Art Institute of Chicago**, stocked with treasures bestowed by civic-minded 19th-century collectors, to the natural history curiosities of the **Field Museum** and the scientific wonders of the **Museum of Science and Industry**. The arts come alive nightly in more than 200 theaters and many jazz and blues clubs in town.

Whether you are visiting for a weekend or longer, our Top 10 guide distills the best of Chicago, from the hidden neighborhood pub to the bustling **Magnificent Mile**. There are tips for the best freebies and tours, places to take the kids and dine memorably, plus seven easy-to-follow itineraries, designed to make the most use of your time in the city. Add inspiring photography and detailed maps, and you've got the essential pocket-sized travel companion. **Enjoy the book, and enjoy Chicago.**

Clockwise from top: **Chicago skyline; lion statues outside the Art Institute of Chicago; Sue, the** *Tyrannosaurus rex* **exhibit at the Field Museum; Arthur Heurtley House, Oak Park; window at the Richard H. Driehaus Gallery of Stained Glass; Jay Pritzker Pavilion, Millennium Park; Botanic Garden**

Exploring Chicago

Thanks to a convenient concentration of attractions, it is easy to cram Chicago's highlights into a few days, or even a weekend. The following two- and four-day itineraries are packed with ideas for you to make the most of your visit, and to fully immerse yourself in the city's sights, sounds, and flavors.

Magnificent Mile is a great, bustling shopping experience.

Two Days in Chicago

Day ❶
MORNING
Take a **Chicago Architecture Foundation** cruise (see p115) along the Chicago River to get an overview of the city's design prowess. Walk a few blocks south to explore **Millennium Park** (see pp34–5).
AFTERNOON
Take the bridge from the park to the **Art Institute of Chicago** (see pp14–17) to admire the Impressionist collection. See the city on high from nearby **Willis Tower** (see pp12–13), indulge in pizza at **Uno's** (see p61), and then catch a comedy show at **Second City** (see p55).

Day ❷
MORNING
Start your day with a visit to the **John G. Shedd Aquarium** (see pp28–9) – if you book online in advance you can skip the line. Afterward, cross the Museum Campus to the famous **Field Museum** (see pp18–19).

AFTERNOON
Make your way to **Navy Pier** (see pp24–5) for a whirl on some of the carnival rides. Then hit retail magnet, **Magnificent Mile** (see pp32–3). Finish up at a jazz or blues club (see pp56–7).

Four Days in Chicago

Day ❶
MORNING
Sign up for the **Chicago Architecture Foundation** (see p115) river cruise and disembark at Michigan Avenue. Walk up the **Magnificent Mile** (see pp32–3) to take in the pulse of the city.
AFTERNOON
After lunch at **Spiaggia** (see p83), continue northward for a stroll in the leafy **Lincoln Park Zoo** (see pp30–31).

Day ❷
MORNING
Browse the vast collections of the **Art Institute of Chicago** (see pp14–15). Take the bridge from the Modern Wing into **Millennium Park** (see pp34–5), and grab lunch at **Park Grill** (see pp34–5).

Aviation exhibit at the **Museum of Science and Industry**

Willis Tower is the tallest building in Chicago.

Key
— Two-day itinerary
— Four-day itinerary

Spiaggia

Magnificent Mile

Lake Shore Park

STREETERVILLE

Michigan Avenue

Navy Pier

Chicago Shakespeare Theater

See inset, left

To Second City (2 miles)

Chicago

River

CTA GREEN LINE

See inset, left

Chicago Architecture Foundation Cruise

Millennium Park Station

Millennium Park

DOWNTOWN

Park Grill

Art Institute of Chicago

Willis Tower

Buckingham Fountain

METRA TRAIN

Navy Pier is a leisure playground for all ages.

Grant Park

SOUTH SIDE

John G. Shedd Aquarium

Field Museum

See inset, left

0 meters 500
0 yards 500

AFTERNOON
Take a trip on the CTA Green Line "L" out to **Oak Park** *(see pp36–7)* to see architect Frank Lloyd Wright's former home and studio. On the return, get off in the Loop to hit one of the many restaurants and bars in the area *(see p77).*

Day ❸
MORNING
Start at the **John G. Shedd Aquarium** *(see pp28–9)*, then cross the Museum Campus to marvel at Sue, the giant *Tyrannosaurus rex* on display at the **Field Museum** *(see pp18–19).*

AFTERNOON
Admire the city from aloft at the **Willis Tower** *(see pp12–13)*. Then visit **Navy Pier** *(see pp24–5)* for a lake cruise, dinner, and a performance at **Chicago Shakespeare Theater** *(see pp25 & 55).*

Day ❹
MORNING
Spend the morning exploring the many exhibits of the **Museum of Science and Industry** *(see pp20–21)* in Hyde Park, including the coal mine and German WWII submarine.

AFTERNOON
Have lunch at **Valois** cafeteria *(see p105)*, then take the Metra train to **Millennium Park** *(see pp34–5)*. Rent a Divvy bicycle and ride the **Lakefront Recreational Path** *(see p64)*. After dark, stroll around the illuminated **Buckingham Fountain** *(see p72).*

Top 10 Chicago Highlights

The futuristic Jay Pritzker Pavilion in Millennium Park

Chicago Highlights	**10**		John G. Shedd Aquarium	**28**
Willis Tower and Its Views	**12**		Lincoln Park Zoo	**30**
The Art Institute of Chicago	**14**		Magnificent Mile	**32**
Field Museum	**18**		Millennium Park	**34**
Museum of Science and Industry	**20**		Frank Lloyd Wright's Oak Park	**36**
Navy Pier	**24**			

🔟 Chicago Highlights

Big-city sophistication combined with small-town hospitality create the perfect blend in this, the Midwest's largest city. Chicago's architecture, cuisine for all budgets and taste, great shopping, diverse ethnic neighborhoods, outstanding museums, and a lakefront setting make this an exciting place to visit.

❶ Willis Tower and Its Views

The city's skyscraping superlative is actually made up of nine tube-like sections. The views are awesome: on a clear day, you can see up to 40 miles (64 km) from the 103rd-floor Skydeck *(see pp12–13).*

❷ The Art Institute of Chicago

This grande dame of Chicago's art scene features world-renowned collections. The Impressionist section is outstanding *(see pp14–17).*

❸ Field Museum

Delve into cultures and environments from ancient Egypt to modern Africa, via Midwestern wildlife, and the underground life of bugs. The Field also offers a closeup of the world's largest and most complete *Tyrannosaurus rex* skeleton *(see pp18–19).*

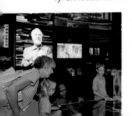

❹ Museum of Science and Industry

This museum is the only building left from the 1893 World's Columbian Exposition. Interactive exhibits range from space exploration to coal mining, including a ride on the Silver Streak train *(see pp20–21).*

5 **Navy Pier**
Once a tourist trap, this Lake Michigan pier is now a bustling year-round playground. In warm weather, take a boat tour or join the throngs that stroll along the pier and get some amazing city views *(see pp24–5)*.

John G. Shedd Aquarium **6**
Chicago's aquarium on the lakefront houses thousands of marine animals, from big beluga whales to tiny seahorses. Get a fish-eye view at the Oceanarium's underwater viewing galleries *(see pp28–9)*.

7 **Lincoln Park Zoo**
It might not be the biggest but it's one of the oldest zoos in the country. Kids love the viewing gallery at the Polar Bear Pool and the AT&T Endangered Species Carousel *(see pp30–31)*.

8 **Magnificent Mile**
Chicago's premier shopping destination is a four-lane stretch of North Michigan Avenue. It also claims two of only a few structures to survive the 1871 Great Chicago Fire *(see pp32–3)*.

9 **Millennium Park**
Opened in 2004, Millennium Park has many attractions that are a magnet for locals and visitors alike *(see pp34–5)*.

10 **Frank Lloyd Wright's Oak Park**
Frank Lloyd Wright, creator of Prairie Style architecture, was based in this Chicago suburb for 20 years. His legacy is an "outdoor museum" of 25 buildings. Take a self-guided or guided tour of his creations *(see pp36–7)*.

Greater Chicago

NORTHSIDE

Oak Park
CENTRAL AVE
NORTH AVE
EISENHOWER EXPRESSWAY
WESTERN AVENUE
CICERO
area of map left
STEVENSON EXPRESSWAY
DAN RYAN EXPWY
FAR SOUTH

0 km   5
0 miles   5

STREET
STREET
STREET
AVENUE
NORTH LAKE SHORE DRIVE
Navy Pier Park
Gateway Park

River
WACKER DRIVE
RANDOLPH STREET
Monroe Harbor

SOUTH LAKE SHORE DRIVE
Lake Michigan
Museum Campus

TOP10 ⭐ Willis Tower and Its Views

It might have lost the US's tallest building slot, but Willis Tower is still the second tallest in the country, at 1,450 ft (442 m). Designed by Chicago firm Skidmore, Owings & Merrill, the tower uses nine exterior frame tubes, avoiding the need for interior supports. For awesome 360-degree views of the city, head to the 103rd-floor Skydeck, where the brave can also step into a series of glass boxes that provide fascinating views straight down to the ground.

1 John Hancock Center
The Willis Tower's North Side counterpart is this 100-story skyscraper. It houses a retail area, offices, and apartments – as well as an open-air observatory *(see p79)*.

2 Soldier Field
Home to the Chicago Bears football team *(see p67)* for over 30 years, the lakeside stadium **(above)**, which opened in 1924, saw the addition of a 67,000-seat structure in 2003.

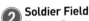

3 Marina City
When built in 1964, these 60-story buildings **(left)**, nicknamed the corncobs, were once the tallest residential structures in the world *(see p42)*.

NEED TO KNOW

MAP J4 ■ 233 S. Wacker Dr. (entrance on Jackson Blvd.) ■ "L" Station: Quincy/Wells ■ 312-875-9696 ■ www.theskydeck.com ■ www.willistower.com

Open Apr–Sep: 9am–10pm; Oct–Mar: 10am–8pm

Adm: Skydeck: $17; children (3–11): $11 ■ DA

Marina City: 300 N. State St.

Soldier Field: 425 E. McFetridge Dr.

United Center: 1901 W. Madison St.

McCormick Place: 2301 S. Lake Shore Dr.

■ The tower has eight restaurants to pick from.

■ Take an audio Sky Tour for information on Chicago at the Skydeck's 16 viewing points.

■ Check visibility levels at the security desk before you wait in line for the Skydeck.

4 **Chicago River**
Chicago's 156-mile- (250-km-) long river tops world records with its 43 opening bridges. An amazing engineering feat resulted in the reversal of the river flow in 1900 (see p40). Every St. Patrick's Day the main branch is dyed green.

7 **Lake Michigan**
This is the third largest of the five Great Lakes. Water temperatures struggle to hit tepid during summer, but many beach-goers swim nevertheless. On a clear day, you can often see across to the shores of Indiana and Michigan.

TOP 10 TOWER FACTS
1 It is 110 stories high
2 It weighs a massive 222,500 tons
3 The tower took three years to construct
4 Building costs topped $150 million
5 It contains over 2,000 miles (3,220 km) of electric cables …
6 … And 25,000 miles (40,233 km) of piping
7 25,000 people enter and exit each day
8 1.3 million visit the Skydeck each year
9 The elevators travel at an ear-popping 1,600 ft (490 m) per minute
10 Six automatic machines wash its 16,100 windows

Willis Tower dominating the Chicago skyline

5 **United Center**
This vast indoor sports arena and concert venue is also known as "the house that Michael built," as it was basketball player Michael Jordan's fame that attracted the money to fund it. Outside, there's a statue of him.

8 **Merchandise Mart**
One of the world's largest commercial buildings (in floor area), this 1930s structure was run by the Kennedy family until the late 1990s (see p79).

9 **McCormick Place**
The first convention center opened here in 1960 but burned down seven years later. Helmut Jahn built the second in 1971 at twice the size with 40,000 sprinkler heads. Four buildings now make up this complex, and are connected by a shop-lined promenade.

10 **Navy Pier**
A former naval base turned fun-filled mecca, and Chicago's top attraction (see pp24–5).

6 **Grant Park**
Built entirely on landfill following the Great Chicago Fire (see p40), this 319-acre park **(right)** is one of the city's largest and the site of summer music festivals (see p46).

TOP10 ⭐ The Art Institute of Chicago

Guarded by iconic lions and up a flight of grand stone steps is the Midwest's largest art museum. Housed in a massive Beaux-Arts edifice with an impressive Modern Wing by Renzo Piano, the Institute has some 260,000 works from around the globe, and is famous for its Impressionist and Post-Impressionist collections.

③ Nighthawks
One of the best-known images in 20th-century American art, this 1942 painting **(left)** by Realist Edward Hopper has a melancholy quality. It includes a depiction of fluorescent lighting, new at the time to US cities.

① Acrobats at the Cirque Fernando
Children were often the subjects of Renoir's sunny paintings: this luminous 1879 work shows a circus owner's daughters taking a bow after their act.

④ The Old Guitarist
A young, struggling Picasso painted this tortured 1903 portrait during his Blue Period. It reflected his grief over a friend's suicide and was a precursor to his own style of Cubism.

American Gothic ②

Grant Wood borrowed from the detailed style of Flemish Renaissance art to create this painting (1930). Though perceived by many as satirical, the painting **(right)** celebrates rural American values.

⑤ Stacks of Wheat Series
From 1890 to 1891, Monet painted 30 views of the haystacks that stood outside his house in France. This museum has six, which illustrate the Impressionist doctrine of capturing the fleeting effects of light in nature.

NEED TO KNOW

MAP L4 ▪ 111 S. Michigan Ave ▪ "L" Station: Adams (Green, Orange, Purple, Brown & Pink lines), Monroe (Blue & Red lines) ▪ 312-443-3600 ▪ www.artic.edu

Open 10:30am–5pm Mon–Fri (to 8pm Thu); 10:30am–5pm Sat & Sun

Adm: adults $25; students, seniors and children 14 yrs and older $19; under-14s free; free adm 1st and 2nd Wed of month, 5–8pm Thu, 5–9pm summer, and Feb ▪ DA

▪ Terzo Piano (Modern Wing) is perfect for a fine-dining lunch with city views, or cross over to GePaDe Caffe (60 E. Adams St.) for great panini.

▪ Join a free, hour-long introductory tour. Meet in gallery 100 (noon daily, and 2pm Tue, Wed, and Fri).

▪ Don't miss the reconstruction of the 1893 Stock Exchange Trading Room.

Museum Guide
The Art Institute is the second-largest art museum in the US. Locations of works and accessibility of specific galleries are subject to change; if there is a particular work you want to see, check in advance to ensure it is on view.

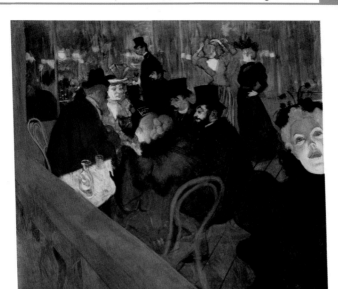

6 **At the Moulin Rouge**

Unlike many of his fellow Impressionists who painted serene scenes, Toulouse-Lautrec was drawn to the exuberant nightlife of Paris. This dramatic painting (1892) celebrates the Moulin Rouge cabaret **(above)**.

8 **America Windows**

Unveiled at the Art Institute in 1977, Marc Chagall's stunning stained-glass windows were a gift to the city he loved. The six vibrant panels depict the US as a place of cultural and religious freedom.

10 **The Herring Net**

Winslow Homer honed his Realist skills as an illustrator for magazines. After moving to Maine, he created a series of images, including this one (1885), depicting man's complex relationship with the sea.

7 **A Sunday on La Grande Jatte – 1884**

Massive and mesmerizing, this painting took Georges Seurat two years to complete. The scene is created from dots of color, based on his study of optical theory, later known as pointillism.

Key to Floorplan
- Lower level
- First level
- Second level
- Third level

9 **The Child's Bath**

The only American to exhibit in Paris with the Impressionists, Mary Cassatt often portrayed women and children as in this **(left)**, her most famous painting (1893). Her domestic subjects reflect the limited freedom of women at the time.

🔟 Collections

Two Sisters, by Pierre August Renoir, a highlight of the European Collection

1 European Collection

Arranged chronologically, and spanning the Middle Ages through 1950, this prodigious collection includes a significant array of Renaissance and Baroque art and sculpture. However, its main draw is a body of nearly 400 Impressionist and Post-Impressionist paintings. Instrumental in its creation was Bertha Honoré Palmer who acquired over 40 Impressionist works (largely ignored in France at the time) for the 1893 World's Columbian Exposition.

2 American Arts

This impressive holding contains some 5,500 paintings and sculptures dating from the colonial period to 1950. In addition, paintings and works on paper are on loan from the Terra collection, and there is a range of decorative arts, including furniture, glass, and ceramics from the 18th century through to the present. The silver collection is especially noteworthy.

3 Arthur Rubloff Collection of Paperweights

This fabulous and unusual assemblage numbers in excess of 1,400 paperweights, making it one of the largest of its kind in the world. It showcases colorful and exquisite examples from all periods, designs, and techniques. The paperweights mostly originate from 19th-century France, though some were made in America and the United Kingdom. Displays also reveal the secrets of how paperweights are made.

Arthur Rubloff paperweight

4 African and Amerindian Art

A wide variety of artifacts, including sculptures, ceramics, furniture, textiles, masks, jewelry, beadwork, and metalwork, make up this relatively small, but interesting

African and Amerindian exhibits

collection. Exhibits from both continents are arranged by region and culture: ceremonial and ritual objects are particularly intriguing.

5 Architecture

Given the city's strong architectural heritage and focus, it is not surprising that Chicago's Art Institute boasts an architecture and design department, one of only a few in the US. Sketches and drawings are accessible by appointment, and changing public displays feature models, drawings, and architectural pieces, such as a stained-glass window by Frank Lloyd Wright.

6 Modern and Contemporary Art

This important collection represents the significant art movements in Europe and the US from 1950 to the present day, including a strong body of Surrealist works, and paintings by Picasso, Matisse, and Kandinsky, as well as showing how American artists, such as Georgia O'Keeffe, interpreted European Modernism.

7 Thorne Miniature Rooms

Narcissa Ward Thorne, a Chicago art patron, combined her love of miniatures with her interest in interiors and decorative arts to create the 68 rooms in this unique Lilliputian installation. Some of the 1 inch:1 foot scale rooms are replicas of specific historic interiors, while others are

Museum Floorplan

One of Thorne's miniature rooms

period recreations, combining features copied from a variety of sites or based on illustrations and other records of period furniture.

8 Photography

Spanning the history of the medium, from its origins in 1839 to the present, this eminent collection was started by Georgia O'Keeffe in 1949 with the donation of works by Alfred Stieglitz. Many modern masters, including Julien Levy, Edward Weston, Paul Strand, and Eugène Atget, are represented.

9 Asian Art

This sizeable collection covers 5,000 years and features Chinese ceramics and jades, Japanese screens, and Southeast Asian sculpture. The museum's assemblage of Japanese woodblock prints, such as *Courtesan* (c.1705–1715) by Kaigetsudo Dohan, is one of the most impressive outside Japan. Look out, too, for the rare early 14th-century scroll painting, *Legends of the Yuzu Nembutsu Sect*.

10 Arms and Armor

The Harding Collection of Arms and Armor is one of the largest in America. On permanent display are over 200 items related to the art of war, including weapons, and complete and partial suits of armor for men – as well as horses. The items displayed originate from Europe, the United States, and the Middle East, and date from the 15th through the 19th centuries.

TOP 10 ⭐ Field Museum

Founded in 1893 to display items from the World's Columbian Exposition, and renamed in 1905 to honor its first major benefactor, Marshall Field, this vast museum offers fascinating insights into global cultures and environments past and present. Home to all sorts of cultural treasures, fossils, and artifacts, as well as to myriad interactive exhibits, make no bones about it: this natural history museum is one of the best in the country.

Sue ①

A *Tyrannosaurus rex* **(right)**, 13-ft (4-m) high by 42-ft (12.8-m) long – the largest, most complete, and best preserved ever found. Her real 600-lb (272-kg) skull is on view nearby.

② Crown Family PlayLab

Six themed areas, from a scientist's lab to a dinosaur dig, are full of things for kids to discover.

③ Grainger Hall of Gems

Fiber-optic lighting magically illuminates over 500 glittering gems, precious stones, and minerals. Even though it's a replica, the star of the show is the breathtaking Hope Diamond **(left)**.

NEED TO KNOW

MAP L6 ■ 1400 S. Lake Shore Dr. ■ Metra station: Roosevelt Rd.
■ 312-922-9410
■ www.fieldmuseum.org

Open 9am–5pm daily
Adm: adults $22, children (3–11) $15, seniors and students with ID $19 ■ DA

■ Grab a bite to eat under the watchful gaze of dinosaur Sue at the Corner Bakery (main level).

■ Two free trolley services link the Field, the Shedd *(see pp28–9)*, and the Art Institute *(see pp16–17)* with the nearest Metra and CTA stations and downtown.

■ Have a museum-related question? Look out for attendants carrying a big "Ask Me" sign.

Museum Guide
The main entrance is located on the museum's north side, though visitors typically enter on the south, where buses, trolleys, and cabs drop off. A third (first level) west entrance is suitable for wheelchair access. If you visit on a weekday, it's worth asking staff about the museum's Free Highlights Tours, which take place twice daily. And don't forget to look for information on the day's special events, tours, and activities, posted throughout the building.

4 Inside Ancient Egypt

This part-original, part-replica Egyptian ruin leads you up and down stairs, into Egyptian bedrooms and tombs, and through a market-place. See how Cleopatra lived and how mummies were wrapped.

7 Africa

Browse the wares of a Saharan market, experience life on a slave ship, and see a pair of fighting elephants: this exhibit offers an amazing and educational journey through ancient and modern Africa for all ages **(right)**.

8 Pacific Spirits

A celebration of vibrant Pacific islander culture: visitors can see dramatic masks, listen to recorded sounds from the swamps of New Guinea, and bang on an impressive 9-ft (3-m) drum.

9 Evolving Planet

Journey through four billion years of life on Earth as a wide range of displays tell the story of evolution. Interact with single-celled organisms, giant dinosaurs, and our first human ancestors.

Key to Floorplan
- First level
- Main level
- Upper level

5 Lions of Tsavo

In 1898, these two partners in crime killed and ate 140 men who were constructing a bridge in Kenya, before they in turn were hunted and killed. The skins were first used as rugs, before being mounted as you see today.

10 The Ancient Americas

Step into the world of Ice Age mammoth-hunters, enter an 800-year-old pueblo, and explore the Aztec Empire, as artifacts **(left)** and displays uncover 13,000 years of human history in the Americas.

6 Underground Adventure

Enter this larger-than-life "subterranean" ecosystem to get a bug's-eye view of life. Wander through a jungle of roots **(right)**, and listen to the chatter of a busy ant colony. Extra admission charged.

🔟 ⭐ Museum of Science and Industry

The cultural star of the city's Far South, this museum was the first in North America to introduce interactive exhibits, with a record of innovative, hands-on displays dating back to the 1930s. More than one million visitors flock annually to this vast Neo-Classical building, which houses more than 800 exhibits and is a Chicago must-see, especially for families. Make sure you arrive rested, since it takes a whole day to hit just the top attractions.

1 Henry Crown Space Center

This, the first manned spacecraft to orbit the moon, offers a peek into the 1960s space race. Historic photos, space suits, and a training module set the scene.

2 Science Storms

This two-story exhibit (above) illustrates basic principles of physics and chemistry using recreations of natural phenomena, including a 40-ft (12-m) tornado, a giant Tesla coil that produces lighting, and a 30-ft (9-m) wave tank.

3 Coal Mine

Venture down a simulated 600 ft (184 m) in an authentic shaft elevator to discover how coal was extracted in the 1930s compared to today. The mini train ride enhances the underground illusion.

4 Omnimax Theater

The films shown in this five-story theater make the viewers feel like they are right in the thick of the on-screen action and adventures. On a rotating program, the films are screened approximately every 50 minutes.

5 YOU! The Experience

Discover aspects of the human body and mind from a new perspective. The centerpiece of this exhibit is the giant 13-ft (4-m-) tall animated 3-D human heart, which offers a fascinating interactive experience.

7 ToyMaker 3000

Twelve robotic arms work the assembly line to produce toy top after colorful top in this display of computer integrated manufacturing technology. Race a robot to see who can trace letters faster, and souvenir tops come free.

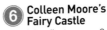

6 Colleen Moore's Fairy Castle

Star of the silent screen, Colleen Moore commissioned the design of this lavish miniature castle, a study in craftsmanship (left), and lovingly filled it with over 2,000 one-twelfth-scaled objects, including the world's smallest Bible.

8 All Aboard the Silver Streak
Both Art Deco design aficionados and rail buffs are drawn to this streamlined, vintage Zephyr train **(above)** with its ground-breaking diesel-electric engine.

Key to Floorplan
- First level
- Main level
- Upper level

10 The Great Train Story
Over 20 miniature trains race past skyscrapers, through prairies, and over the Rockies to the Pacific Docks on 1,425 ft (437 m) of track **(above)** that replicate the 2,200-mile (3,540-km) train trip from Chicago to Seattle on this interactive model railroad.

9 U-505 Submarine
Take a tour around this original 1941 German U-boat **(above)**. The submarine was captured during World War II and still looks much as it did then, complete with an Enigma codebreaking machine.

NEED TO KNOW

MAP F6 ■ 57th St. & Lake Shore Dr. ■ Metra station: 55th/56th/57th Sts. ■ 1-773-684-1414 ■ www.msichicago.org

Open 9:30am–4pm daily

Adm: adults $18, children (3–11) $11, seniors $14; including one Omnimax show: adults $27, children $18, seniors $21 ■ DA

■ The Brain Food Court serves above-average fare, and has a kids' zone.

■ Advance tickets reserved on the Internet or telephone cost extra but are worth it on busy weekends.

■ Additional Omnimax tickets are sold at all museum entrances: adults $8, children (3–11) $6, seniors $7.

Museum Guide
The museum has two main entrances – the Great Hall (first level) and the Henry Crown Space Center (for the Omnimax Theater). Head first to tour-only displays (Silver Streak, U-505, the Coal Mine) as later waits for these can be more than an hour. Visit the Omnimax later – you'll appreciate sitting down. Strollers can be rented in the Great Hall.

🔟 Exhibits

Transportation Gallery

1 Transportation Gallery
A full-size Boeing 727 and a British World War II fighter plane dangle dramatically above a steam locomotive and the world's fastest land vehicle, while visitors explore the forces of flight via engaging computer games and videos.

2 U-505
Artifacts, archival footage, and interactive challenges bring to life this restored U-505 German submarine. Optional on-board tours of the boat are available.

3 Genetics and the Baby Chick Hatchery
Explore the complex and controversial world of genetics and genetic engineering and learn how cloning is possible, while viewing real cloned mice.

4 Farm Tech
Learn about life on today's farms and the modern technologies that get food from the field to your table. Children can ride in a real combine and take part in a cow-milking challenge.

5 Networld
The world of cyberspace comes alive here via educational yet fun hands-on displays.

6 The Art of the Bicycle
This fascinating exhibit explores the pioneering evolution of the bicycle over the last 200 years.

7 Ships Through the Ages
Here, model ships chart marine transportation from Egyptian sailboats through to modern ocean liners. Highlights include scale versions of Christopher Columbus's three ships.

8 The Swiss Jolly Ball
The world's largest pinball machine has been here since 1998. Watch the pinball race through Swiss-themed scenery and admire its complicated mechanics.

9 Communications Zone
The Whispering Gallery shows how sound waves make the faintest whisper audible at the other end of a room, while THINK explores the working relationship between people and technology.

10 Poop Happens
In this one-of-a-kind science theater show, viewers follow food right the way through the digestive process, from the mouth to the stomach – and beyond.

Museum Floorplan

THE MUSEUM'S ORIGINS

Ferris Wheel

Built as the Palace of Fine Arts in 1893, the Museum of Science and Industry is the only building left from Daniel Burnham's "White City." This was built for the World's Columbian Exposition, marking the 400th anniversary (albeit one year late) of Christopher Columbus's arrival in the New World. Burnham, the Director of Works for the fair *(see p43)*, commissioned architects like Charles Atwood to create structures that would showcase the best in design, culture, and technology. The Field Museum *(see pp18–19)* inhabited the building until the 1920s when it moved to its Museum Campus home. Sears Roebuck retail chief Julius Rosenwald then decided that a fortified palace, stripped to its steel frame and rebuilt in limestone, would be the perfect home for a new museum devoted to "industrial enlightenment" and US technological triumphs. The Museum launched around 1933 when Chicago hosted its next World's Fair, Century of Progress Exposition.

TOP 10 FEATURES OF THE 1893 EXPOSITION

1 First ever Ferris Wheel
2 Palace of Fine Arts
3 Midway Plaisance, first separate amusement area at a world's fair
4 Jackson Park, landscaped by designer Frederick Law Olmsted
5 Exotic Dancer "Little Egypt" in the "Streets of Cairo" exhibit
6 The nickname "Windy City" was introduced *(see p113)*
7 A 1,500 lb (680 kg) chocolate Venus de Milo
8 A 70-ft- (21-m-) high tower of light bulbs
9 Floodlights used on buildings for the first time
10 250,000 separate displays on show

The Museum of Science and Industry building started out as the Palace of Fine Arts in 1893.

Present-day Museum of Science and Industry building

TOP 10 ⭐ Navy Pier

Back in 1995, Chicago's Navy Pier was a drab slab of concrete projecting into Lake Michigan, formerly used as a military and freight terminal. But a huge effort to attract locals and tourists resulted in the installation of a variety of attractions on the waterfront – for kids as well as adults – that draw over nine million people annually, making this Chicago's most visited attraction. The Pier underwent extensive renovations for its 100th anniversary in 2016.

4 Musical Carousel

A quaint merry-go-round of 36 hand-painted horses and chariots next to the Ferris Wheel replicates a similar ride installed on the Pier in the 1920s.

5 Centennial Wheel

It's hard to miss the Pier's 196-ft- (60-m-) high ferris wheel **(right)**, installed in 2016 to replace its smaller predecessor. The slowly revolving ride seats eight in each of its 42 enclosed cars. Daytime rides offer fine lake views, while at night, light shows projected onto the wheel create colorful displays.

1 Wave Swinger

Each of the 48 chain-suspended chairs on this colorful, old-fashioned thrill ride lifts riders 14 ft (5 m) in the air, and spins them until the skyline blurs **(above)**.

2 IMAX® Theatre

The six-story movie theater offers celluloid fare ranging from scientific documentaries to Disney features. Sound and vision headsets aid 3-D movie fun.

3 Polk Bros Park

Navy Pier's front yard is marked by a dramatic fountain with around 250 programmable jets that mimic the movement of water, schools of fish, or flocks of birds. In winter, the park converts into an ice rink.

6 New Food Experience

Replacing run-of-the-mill boardwalk fare, the Pier's newly revamped food court includes several satellites of Chicago-based restaurants such as the two North Side favorites, DMK Burger Bar and Fish Bar.

7 Chicago Children's Museum

Kids love this hands-on museum **(below)** that educates through play. Under-twos get dedicated spaces, including a water room *(see p52)*.

Navy Pier Plan ③ ② ① ⑥ ⑨ ⑩

⑦ ④ ⑤ ⑧

■ Skip the chain eateries for ribs and live jazz at Joe's Be-Bop Café.

■ In summer the beer garden at the far end of the Pier has stellar city views and free bands.

■ Join a 90-minute lake tour *(see p114)* on a four-masted schooner, or take a ride on a Seadog speedboat.

■ Save money and time spent waiting in line by purchasing a combination ticket for the Musical Carousel, Centennial Wheel, and Wave Swinger.

Orientation
Take public transit, a taxi, or walk to Navy Pier. If driving, you'll find over 1,600 parking spaces right on the Pier. Once there, be sure to stop off at the Guest Services desk, just inside the main entrance, to pick up a schedule for details of the day's events, including performance times and locations for the resident comedy troupe, brass band, and a capella singing group.

⑧ Chicago Shakespeare Theater

This highly respected theater aims to make the Bard accessible to the pleasure-seeking masses visiting Navy Pier. As well as the Shakespearean standards performed here, productions also include the "Short Shakespeare" series for younger audiences.

⑨ Amazing Chicago's Funhouse Maze

This mirror-filled, Chicago-themed walking maze leads you on a disorienting, 15-minute journey. Expect spinning lights, startling sound effects, and new perspectives on the city's history and sights. It is an ideal rainy-day attraction.

Richard H. Driehaus ⑩ Gallery of Stained Glass

This free-admission gallery features 11 stained-glass windows **(right)** by decorative arts master Louis Comfort Tiffany. Examples include illuminated windows depicting religious, landscape, and figurative scenes (many saved from Gilded Age mansions).

Following pages Aerial view across the city to Lake Michigan

TOP 10 ★ John G. Shedd Aquarium

The eponymous John G. Shedd, president of Marshall Field's department store (see p76), donated this Beaux-Arts aquarium to Chicago in 1929. One of the city's top attractions, it houses some 25,500 marine animals representing 2,100 different species that include amphibians, fish, and aquatic mammals. The latter can be seen in the saltwater of the glass-walled Oceanarium, which places an infinity pool in front of Lake Michigan to transporting effect.

1 Caribbean Reef

This vibrant tropical tank **(left)** contains glinting tarpon, bonnethead sharks, fluttering rays, and many other fish. A scuba diver hand-feeds them six times daily, narrating his task via an underwater microphone.

2 Stingray Touch

Dip your hand into the cool, shallow pool filled with stingrays to feel their smooth and muscular wings. The exhibit is the aquarium's first outdoor installation, and therefore closed in winter. Staff manning the pool provide animal interpretation.

3 Animal Enounters

Get up close and personal with Chilean rose tarantulas, African bullfrogs, and red-tailed boas in handler-controlled encounters, held hourly.

4 Waters of the World

Themed tanks hold over 90 re-created aquatic habitats, including Ocean Coasts, Tropical Waters, and Africa, Asia, and Australia. An Australian lungfish, known as "Granddad," has been a resident since 1933.

5 Wild Reef

Gain a daring diver's perspective of whitetip reef, blacktip reef, sand-bar, and zebra sharks **(above)**. The sawfish and fearsome lionfish happily hold their own amid the predator school.

Exterior view of the Shedd

NEED TO KNOW

MAP M6 ▪ 1200 S. Lake Shore Dr. ▪ "L" station: Roosevelt (Green, Orange, & Red lines) ▪ 312-939-2438 ▪ www.shedd aquarium.org

Open summer (Memorial Day to Labor Day): 9am–6pm daily (to 10pm Thu Jun–Aug); winter: 9am–5pm Mon–Fri, 9am–6pm Sat & Sun

▪ Adm: adults $8; children (3–11) & seniors $6; aquatic show an additional $2 ▪ DA

▪ Choose one of three dining options at the Shedd: the Soundings serves upscale fare with lake views; the Bubble Net Food Court offers pizzas, sandwiches, and burgers; the Deep Ocean Café offers kid-friendly fare such as hot dogs and mac 'n' cheese.

▪ Don't miss the underwater viewing galleries.

▪ Check out Jazzin' at the Shedd on Thursdays (5–10pm, adm $20) from June through August.

Aquarium Guide
Consult the day's event schedule printed on the map you're given. Arrive 10–15 minutes early for an Oceanarium Show to get the best seats, and remember that the 20–30-minute Habitat Chats often follow on after the shows.

6 Special Exhibit Gallery

This 3,600-sq-ft (334-sq-m) special exhibit gallery is on the mezzanine level of the Oceanarium and features changing exhibits focused on aquatic animals.

7 4-D Experience

This hi-tech theater experience has "special FX seats" that bombard spectators with bubbles, wind, smells, sounds, and other surprises.

8 Amazon Rising

Demonstrating the huge seasonal tides of the world's longest river, this exhibit presents a year in the life of the Amazon flood plain. Look out for the piranha.

9 Habitat Chats

Oceanarium staffers hold daily discussions about the beluga whales, sea otters, and rockhopper penguins in their charge. Twice daily chats also cover a changing roster of fish at the aquarium.

10 Abbott Oceanarium

Underwater galleries **(left)** afford incredible views of the likes of dolphins and beluga whales swimming through the Oceanarium's vast pools. It is bordered by rocky outcrops and towering pines in a re-creation of the Pacific Northwest coast.

Aquarium Plan

TOP 10 ⭐ Lincoln Park Zoo

Chicago's second most popular attraction after Navy Pier, this menagerie is not only one of the oldest zoos in the country but also one of the last not to charge admission. Established in 1868 with just a pair of swans, the zoo has become an important part of the surrounding North Side community. While small compared to many top US zoos, it is a leading light for ape research, and its park setting, duck ponds, historic café, and landmark red barn endear it to all who visit.

3 Polar Bear Pool

The highlight of this pool is the underwater viewing window (left) through which zoo-goers can spy the beautiful sibling bears pawing their way through the water.

4 Regenstein Macaque Forest

A troop of snow monkeys imported from Japan inhabit this forest, which includes treetops for climbing and hot springs.

1 Bird House

Here, a series of habitats showcase their native bird species. And a walk-through tropical aviary allows you to have a close encounter with 20 endangered and exotic species, such as the fairy bluebird, masked lovebird, and green aracari.

2 AT&T Endangered Species Carousel

Ride an artisan-crafted wooden tiger or a bamboo-munching panda on this tent-topped merry-go-round. The carousel is devoted to almost 50 endangered species, many of which are represented in the zoo itself. Admission is charged for this attraction.

5 Regenstein Small Mammal-Reptile House

Replicating the warm climes of South America, Asia, Africa, and Australia, this exhibit introduces the exotic worlds of animals such as snakes (right).

6 Regenstein African Journey

Elephants, rhinos (below), hippos, and giraffes are among the many animals to roam this expansive exhibit. Totally immerse yourself in the sights and sounds of the varied African landscape around you.

7 Kolver Sea Lion Pool

Despite the name, harbor and gray seals inhabit this pool. Visitors can watch them play at the pool's edge or through an underground viewing window. Try to catch the 2pm training and feeding session.

8 Farm-in-the-Zoo

Keeping city kids in touch with their Midwestern roots, this exhibit offers a daily roster of activities such as goat-milking, cow-feeding, and butter-churning, and the chance to see chicks being born.

Lincoln Park Zoo Plan

9 Kolver Lion House

This 1912 structure stands out not only for its grand architecture but also the grand inhabitants. Many kinds of big cats, including Siberian Tigers (left), prowl – and roar – both inside the hall and in outdoor enclosures.

10 Regenstein Center for African Apes

Simulating the natural habitat of chimps and gorillas (below), this exhibit has huge indoor, tri-level spaces rigged with lifelike trees and vines, as well as an out-door yard for summer.

NEED TO KNOW

MAP F3 ■ 2001 N. Clark St. ■ CTA Bus: 151, 156 ■ 312-742-2000 ■ www.lpzoo.org

Open grounds 7am–6pm daily; buildings summer & fall: 10am–5pm daily (summer: to 6:30pm Sat, Sun & hols); winter: 10am–4:30pm daily

Adm: free but $3 charge for AT&T Endangered Species Carousel and Lionel Train Adventure ■ DA

■ **Check out the Mexican fare year-round at the Park Place Café. In summer, grab a fresh-grilled burger at** the historic Café Brauer, which has a beer garden.

■ Have any animal-related questions? If so, ask staffers at the "Discovery Carts" located all around the zoo.

Visitor Guide
Stop by the Gateway Pavilion (just inside the east gate) when you arrive to pick up a free visitor guide, which has details about feeding times and special events. Staff are on hand here to provide extra information about any new animal arrivals or exhibits. Parking facilities, wheelchairs, lockers, and strollers are also available.

Magnificent Mile

This glitzy strip of stores and striking buildings runs for, you guessed it, about a mile (1.6 km), along North Michigan Avenue. A sharp developer came up with the "magnificent" moniker in 1947, and it has stuck ever since. Often known as the Mag Mile, it is home to big-guns department stores like Neiman Marcus, as well as high-end boutiques such as Tiffany & Co., and popular chain stores. The strip is at its best around Christmas when twinkling trimmings provide welcome relief from the often gray days.

John Hancock Center ①

When this super-sleek 100-story skyscraper was built in 1970, it was the world's tallest building. Exhilarating views of Chicago and beyond (right) are afforded by the 94th-floor observatory and adjoining open-air area, the Skywalk (see p79).

② Hotel InterContinental

Originally built in 1929 as a luxury club for the all-male Shrine association, this amazing hotel (see p116) reveals a range of flamboyant architectural styles in its public spaces. You can take a self-guided tour to see the highlights, including the stunning swimming pool (below) on the 14th floor.

③ Water Tower Place

Housing a busy shopping mall, this complex is one of the world's tallest reinforced concrete buildings. Its 100-plus shops and venues include a branch of Macy's and a Broadway-style theater.

④ The Drake Hotel

This elegant hotel became an instant glamor hotspot when it opened New Year's Eve in 1920. Marilyn Monroe was among the stars who visited. High tea here is a treat (see p117).

BRIDGE TO SUCCESS

The North Michigan Avenue bascule bridge, built in 1920, was the first of its kind in the world. Instrumental in Chicago's northward expansion, it provides a fitting gateway to the city's main retail artery – the Mag Mile. The southwest tower houses the McCormick Tribune Bridgehouse and River Museum, which details the history of the Chicago River and features displays on the interworkings of this landmark drawbridge.

5 Chicago Water Works and Pumping Station
Dwarfed by the surrounding skyscrapers, these structures are among the few that survived the Great Fire of 1871. The water tower **(left)** contains an art gallery, while the pumping station still functions *(see p80)*.

6 American Girl Place
Eager girls and their moms swarm to this palace of little-girliness *(see p82)*, which stocks all kinds of merchandise from the American Girl doll range. Try the store café or attend the praised musical performance.

7 Wrigley Building
The two towers of the former Wrigley headquarters add to Michigan Avenue's exciting skyline. At night, colored lights illuminate them, as they have done since the building first opened in 1921 *(see p49)*.

Magnificent Mile Map

8 Oak Street
The north end of Mag Mile ends at Oak Street, a lane lined in high-end boutiques. This is one of the most expensive retail spaces in the city *(see p62)*.

9 Museum of Contemporary Art Chicago
Off Michigan Avenue, the strip's cultural gem features compelling temporary exhibits, a sculpture garden, and performing arts *(see p79)*.

10 Tribune Tower
The result of a design competition organized by the *Chicago Tribune* newspaper, this Gothic tower **(left)** is both adored and abhorred by locals. Either way, it's a dramatic Mag Mile landmark *(see p80)*.

TOP 10 ⭐ Millennium Park

Designed to celebrate the turn of the 21st century with the reclamation of a former railroad yard in an industrial corner of Grant Park, Millennium Park exceeded its goals in becoming a civic magnet, at least in terms of popularity. Art, architecture, the performing arts, and nature each play a role in the popular park, which hosts summer concerts and special events, and draws visitors year-round to its perennial attractions, led by *Cloud Gate*, its signature sculpture.

Cloud Gate Sculpture ③

Designed by sculptor Anish Kapoor, the work *Cloud Gate* **(right)** resembles an enlarged, reflective kidney bean, prompting its nickname, "The Bean." A selfie taken here in front of the work reflects the surrounding skyline and is Chicago's signature souvenir.

① Crown Fountains

Two 50-ft- (15.2-m-) high glass-block towers **(above)** broadcasting the videotaped faces of Chicago residents – keep watching to see if they blink – comprise the Crown Fountains by Spanish artist Jaume Plensa. In summer it's a popular splash park.

④ Lurie Garden

The 15-ft- (4.6-m-) high "shoulder" hedges edging the Lurie Garden pay homage to the "City of Big Shoulders" cited by Carl Sandburg in his poem *Chicago*. They shelter a delicate perennial garden that is spanned by a hardwood footbridge crossing over shallow water.

⑤ Harris Theater

On the northern fringe of the park, the 1,500-seat state-of-the-art Harris Theater specializes in showcasing music and dance; some 35 Chicago performing arts companies call the Harris home, including Hubbard Street Dance, Music of the Baroque, and Chicago Opera Theater.

Jay Pritzker Pavilion ②

Designed by the architect Frank Gehry, the centerpiece performing arts venue of the park is framed in flying wings of steel **(right)**. A criss-crossing trellis of speaker-supporting steel pipes extends out over the lawn of this huge concert venue.

6 Ice-Skating Rink

The Millennium Park ice-skating rink (left), generally open between December and March (weather permitting), is free, which perhaps accounts for the throngs of skaters here, eager to glide under the "The Bean."

7 Park Grill

The only restaurant in Millennium Park, Park Grill doesn't rest on its location. The quality meals provide the perfect accompaniment to the views of the city skyline, from casual burgers to more upscale fare. In warm weather, tables sprawl out onto the terrace, which serves as the skating rink in winter.

8 Millennium Monument

Anchoring the northwest corner of the park at tree-lined Wrigley Square, a semi-circular peristyle, or row of 40-ft (12-m) Doric-style columns, recall the original classical monument that stood here in the first half of the 20th century. It's now an attractive backdrop to the modern city.

Millennium Park Map

9 Nichols Bridgeway

Architect Renzo Piano, who designed the Modern Wing addition to the Art Institute of Chicago, also worked on this bridge, which gradually rises from the park to the second story of the museum across the street.

10 BP Bridge

The bridge (below) connecting Millennium Park to neighboring Maggie Daley Park (see p52) was designed by Frank Gehry. The steel-clad winding structure offers views of Lake Michigan, the skyline, and Millennium Park, and takes an intentionally indirect route.

NEED TO KNOW

MAP L4 ▪ 201 E. Randolph St. ▪ 312-742-1168 ▪ www.millenniumpark.org

Park: 6am–11pm daily

Welcome Center: 312-742-2963; open May–Sep: 9am–7pm; Oct–Apr: 10am–4pm

▪ There are free 45-minute guided tours twice daily in May–Oct. Ask at the Welcome Center for details.

TOP 10 ⭐ Frank Lloyd Wright's Oak Park

This suburb, 7 miles (11 km) west of downtown Chicago, contains the world's largest collection of Frank Lloyd Wright-designed buildings. It was here that Wright developed his Prairie style (inspired by the flat lines of the Midwestern plains). His work was initially considered radical compared to the typical styles of the day. Walking through Oak Park's quaint, tree-lined streets, it's evident that Wright's architecture stands out from the norm – but in all the right ways.

FRANK LLOYD WRIGHT

After moving to Oak Park in 1889, Wright (1867–1959) appeared to lead the perfect suburban life. But in the early 20th century he caused scandal by gallivanting with married women and wearing flamboyant clothes. During the Depression, he changed into a respected social visionary, and later redefined himself as a quick-witted sage. Ultimately, he established himself as the first celebrity architect.

Unity Temple ②

This compact church (1908) superbly demonstrates Wright's use of poured concrete for both structural and decorative purposes **(right)**.

⑤ Charles Matthews House

Chicago architects Thomas Eddy Tallmadge and Vernon S. Watson designed this elegant 1909 Prairie-style residence for a wealthy pharmacist. Among the notable interior details are Prairie-inspired light fixtures and folding art-glass doors.

③ Frank Lloyd Wright Home and Studio

Built when the famous architect moved to Oak Park (1889), this house **(above)** is where Wright designed over 150 structures. The children's playroom is luminous with signature art-glass windows.

① Beachy House

This impressive 1906 home contradicts many of Wright's trademarks. Instead of just stucco and wood or brick and concrete, he used them all: it also has a seven-gabled, rather than a hipped, roof.

④ Pleasant Home

This 30-room Prairie-style 1897 home **(left)** built by George Maher, was Oak Park's first to have electricity. The 30-room architectural gem holds a small history museum, with exhibits relating to Tarzan creator and former local resident, Edgar Rice Burroughs.

6 Edwin Cheney House

This home sparked a tragic love affair between Wright and Mamah Cheney, leading him to abandon his family and practice. Mamah and her children were murdered at Wright's home by an insane servant in 1914.

7 The Bootleg Houses

Wright lost his job over these three private commissions, built while he was employed by Louis H. Sullivan *(see p43)*. Though Queen Anne-like in style, they hint at the design elements that were to be his hallmarks.

8 Arthur Heurtley House

Wright's beautiful 1902 house **(above)** is absolute Prairie, with its low, wide chimney, and band of art-glass windows that makes the overhanging roof appear to float.

9 Nathan Moore House

Out of financial desperation, Wright built this charming Tudor-style home for his neighbor. After a fire destroyed the top floors in 1922, Wright's modifications echoed his West Coast concrete block houses.

NEED TO KNOW

MAP A4 ■ "L" Station: Oak Park

Frank Lloyd Wright Home & Studio: 951 Chicago Ave.; 312-994-4000; www.gowright.org; open 10am–5pm daily

Unity Temple: 875 West Lake St.

Pleasant Home: 217 South Home Ave.

Arthur Heurtley House: 318 Forest Ave.

The Bootleg Houses: 1019/1027/1031 Chicago Ave.

Charles Matthews House: 432 North Kenilworth Ave.

Edwin Cheney House: 520 North East Ave.

Beachy House: 238 Forest Ave.

Nathan Moore House: 333 Forest Ave.

Harry Adams House: 710 Augusta Blvd.

....

■ The Oak Park Visitors' Center (1010 Lake St.) sells maps, books, and tour tickets.

Oak Park Street Map

10 Harry Adams House

This striking 1913 home marks the last of Wright's Oak Park houses and features several of the elements that made him famous, such as exquisite stained glass, and a low overhanging roof.

The Top 10 of Everything

Stunning spiral staircase, The Rookery, S. LaSalle St.

Moments in Chicago History	**40**	Performing Arts	**54**
Skyscrapers	**42**	Blues and Jazz Joints	**56**
Niche Museums	**44**	Bars and Clubs	**58**
Parks and Beaches	**46**	Places to Eat	**60**
Film Locations	**48**	Shopping Destinations	**62**
Off the Beaten Path	**50**	Chicago for Free	**64**
Kids' Chicago	**52**	Festivals and Events	**66**

🔟 Moments in Chicago History

The Great Chicago Fire of 1871

① 1871: Great Chicago Fire
Over 250 people died and 17,000 buildings were destroyed in this fire, allegedly started by a cow kicking over a lantern. Just a few buildings survived, including the Historic Water Tower and Pumping Station (see p80).

② 1885: First Skyscraper
Though just a measly – by today's standards – nine stories, the Home Insurance Building (now demolished) was the tallest of its time. William Le Baron Jenney achieved this architectural feat by designing the first weight-bearing steel frame. From then on, the only way to go was up.

③ 1886: Haymarket Riot
Wealthy industrialists funded amazing Chicago arts institutions, but their workers toiled long hours in abominable conditions. In May 1886, a labor protest ended in an explosion at Haymarket Square that killed eight policemen and two bystanders. Eight anarchists were convicted of murder, though three were later pardoned for lack of evidence.

④ 1892: First Elevated Train
The first train traveled just 3.6 miles (5.8 km) along tracks built above city-owned alleys (avoiding the need to negotiate with private property owners). By 1893, the line was extended to Jackson Park (see p46) to transport visitors to the World's Columbian Exposition (see p23).

⑤ 1900: Reversal of the Chicago River
With sewage flowing downriver to Lake Michigan, the source of the city's drinking water, thousands of Chicagoans were dying from the contamination. To solve the problem, engineers created a canal that forced the river to flow away from the lake: an extraordinary feat of engineering.

⑥ 1919: Chicago Black Sox Scandal
The Chicago White Sox was a winning baseball team but poorly paid, so players sometimes fixed games, pocketing money from gamblers. After a group of players conspired to lose the 1919 World Series, eight of them were indicted, acquitted for insufficient evidence, but banned for life from baseball – and nicknamed the "Black Sox."

Chicago White Sox baseball team

⑦ 1929: Valentine's Day Massacre
This brutal murder of seven of Al Capone's rival gangsters is one of US history's most notorious massacres. Capone set up a sting that sent George "Bugs" Moran's main men to a nearby garage. There, Capone's henchmen, dressed as police officers, lined them up and

riddled them with bullets. Seven bushes now mark the spot (at Clark Street and Dickens Avenue).

8 1942: First Atom Split

Under the football stands on the campus of the University of Chicago, Enrico Fermi made history. He supervised the creation of a primitive nuclear reactor and took the first major step in understanding how to build an atomic bomb.

Enrico Fermi

9 1955: First McDonald's Franchise Opens

Ray Kroc, a milkshake mixer salesman, changed diets worldwide by convincing Dick and Mac McDonald to franchise their San Bernadino, California burger stand. The original restaurant in Des Plaines – 15 miles (24 km) west of Chicago – is now a museum.

10 2008: Barack Obama Elected President

Chicago had elected its first black mayor, Harold Washington, in 1983, but a new national barrier was vaulted with the 2008 election of Illinois senator Barack Obama as president. Thousands of jubilant voters gathered at the public rally in Grant Park on election night to celebrate the historic event.

Barack Obama wins the 2008 election

TOP 10 CHICAGO RESIDENTS

Benny Goodman

1 Jean Baptiste Point du Sable
Chicago's first non-native settler was an African-American trader who set up camp around 1779.

2 Jane Addams
This social activist (1860–1935) founded Hull House social center *(see p97)* and won a Nobel Peace Prize.

3 Carl Sandburg
One of Chicago's nicknames, "City of the big shoulders," was penned by this author/poet (1878–1967).

4 Al Capone
America's best-known mobster (1899–1947) was Chicago's "Public Enemy Number One" until jailed in 1931 for tax evasion.

5 Ernest Hemingway
Born in Oak Park, this hard-living author (1899–1961) left the suburb of "wide lawns and narrow minds" at age 19.

6 Benny Goodman
Born to Russian-Jewish immigrants, jazz great Goodman (1909–1986) earned the title "King of Swing."

7 Hugh Hefner
Hefner (1926–) is the notorious lothario and founder of *Playboy*, whose first issue sold over 50,000 copies.

8 Curtis Mayfield
Soul musician and social activist (1942–99), Mayfield had his first hit *For Your Precious Love* at the age of 16.

9 Oprah Winfrey
TV's talk-show darling (1954–) filmed in Chicago from 1984 to 2011 and has become an honorary native of the city.

10 Barack Obama
The former US President (1961–) taught at the Chicago Law School from 1992 to 2004. His residential home is in the Kenwood neighborhood.

🔟 Skyscrapers

① The Rookery
One of the earliest remaining skyscrapers, this 1888 landmark *(see p72)* combines traditional wall-bearing and newer steel-frame construction. The latter made it possible for its architects, Burnham and Root, to design an open interior, with offices set around a central light well.

The 100-story John Hancock Center

② John Hancock Center
The tapering, 100-story John Hancock Center is somewhat overshadowed by the higher Willis Tower but is arguably more distinctive. Designed by Skidmore, Owings & Merrill, who also did the Willis, it features its own observatory on the 94th floor *(see p79)*.

③ Auditorium Theatre
MAP L5 ▪ 50 E. Congress Pkwy.
▪ For tours call 312-341-2389
Built by Adler and Sullivan in 1889, the ornate Auditorium also originally contained a hotel and office building and had one of the first public air-conditioning systems. The revamped 4,000-seat theater boasts near-perfect acoustics.

④ Reliance Building
The steel skeleton on this 1895-built skyscraper allowed it to be wrapped in glass. It offers a fine example of the Chicago window, characterized by a bay window placed between two narrow, double-hung windows. Occupied by the Hotel Burnham *(see p117)* the inside has replicas of original features *(see p74)*.

⑤ 860–80 N. Lake Shore Drive
MAP L2
You might think these two high-rise apartment buildings (1949–51) look like the others along this classy strip. Actually, the others look like these. Architect Mies van der Rohe perfected the "less is more" approach, which so many other architects went on to copy.

⑥ Willis Tower
This soaring tower, built in 1973 for retailer Sears Roebuck and Co. (who have since moved out), can be seen from almost anywhere in the city. Its Skydeck affords sensational views *(see pp12–13)*.

⑦ Marina City
With its twin cylindrical structures (1959–64) on the Chicago River, Marina City *(see p12)* is a "city within a city," containing offices, residences, a theater, and more. The apartments afford spectacular views, but their shape creates some interior decorating challenges.

Marina City

The innovative exterior of Aqua Tower

(8) Aqua Tower
MAP L3 ▪ 225 N. Columbus Dr.
The exterior of the 84-story Aqua Tower appears to undulate due to the varying elevations of the skyscraper's balconies. Architect Jeanne Gang cites the striated limestone outcroppings that are common along Great Lakes shorelines.

(9) Monadnock Building
Constructed in two stages, this Loop edifice represents the evolution of skyscraper architecture. The northern half was built in 1891 using solely wall-bearing construction, while the southern half was built two years later and incorporated the then-emerging steel-frame technology still used today *(see p74)*.

(10) Tribune Tower
Despite the cathedral-like buttresses atop the Tribune Tower, headquarters of the Chicago Tribune, this Neo-Gothic building was only erected in 1925. Its facade contains stones from 120 global landmarks, including China's Great Wall *(see p80)*.

TOP 10 CHICAGO ARCHITECTS

1 William Le Baron Jenney
The "father of the skyscraper" (1832–1907) who designed the first all-metal-framed structure, the Home Insurance Building, in 1885 *(see p40)*.

2 Daniel Burnham
Visionary city planner and architect, Burnham (1846–1912) was the man behind the White City *(see p23)*.

3 William Holabird & Martin Roche
This influential team (Holabird 1854–1923; Roche 1853–1927) developed early Chicago-style skyscrapers including the Marquette Building *(see p74)*.

4 Louis H. Sullivan
The creator (1856–1924) of the "form follows function" doctrine designed according to a building's intended use.

5 Frank Lloyd Wright
Inspired by the wide open spaces of the Midwest, Wright *(see pp36–7)* was the originator of the Prairie style.

6 George Maher
A Prairie School architect (1864–1926) who favored Arts and Crafts motifs.

7 Walter Burley Griffin
Another Prairie-style architect (1876–1937) with a namesake historic district on Chicago's South Side.

8 Ludwig Mies van der Rohe
This minimalist architect (1886–1969) was the creator of the modern glass-and-steel box.

9 Bertrand Goldberg
Goldberg (1913–1997) designed Marina City, which is typical of his curvilinear concrete shapes.

10 Jeanne Gang
Designer of the award-winning Aqua Tower, Gang (1964–) is a contemporary innovator among skyscraper designers.

Frank Lloyd Wright

⬛TOP10 Niche Museums

immigrants, this tiny museum's permanent collection of personal items brought over by early settlers is supplemented by temporary exhibitions on Swedish culture. An interactive children's museum brings the immigrant journey to life.

③ Hellenic Museum and Cultural Center

MAP H5 ▪ 333 S. Halsted St. ▪ 11am–5pm Tue–Fri (to 8pm Thu), 11am–5pm Sat & Sun ▪ Adm: $10; students and seniors $8; members and under-3s free ▪ www.hellenicmuseum.org

Located in the city's Greektown, this museum is dedicated to celebrating Hellenic culture and the Greek immigrant experience in America.

④ National Museum of Mexican Art

MAP B5 ▪ 1852 W. 19th St. ▪ 10am–5pm Tue–Sun ▪ DA ▪ www.nationalmuseumofmexicanart.org

The largest Latino museum in the US explores the culture *sin fronteras* (without boundaries), showing works from Mexican and Mexican-American communities. Pre-Columbian ceramics, Day of the dead candelabras, and prints by Diego Rivera are highlights of the collection.

① Spertus Museum

MAP L6 ▪ 610 S. Michigan Ave. ▪ 10am–5pm Sun, Mon & Wed (to 6pm Thu & 3pm Fri) ▪ DA ▪ www.spertus.edu

From cartoons to ancient Torah scrolls, this museum offers a lively, multifaceted retelling of Jewish history and culture. The museum's Zell Holocaust Memorial was the first such permanent installation in the US.

② Swedish American Museum

MAP B3 ▪ 5211 N. Clark St. ▪ 10am–4pm Tue–Fri, 11am–4pm Sat & Sun ▪ Adm: $4; children, seniors, students $3 ▪ DA ▪ www.swedishamericanmuseum.org

Located in Andersonville, the historic neighborhood of Scandinavian

National Museum of Mexican Art

⑤ DuSable Museum of African American History

Named for Jean Baptiste Point du Sable, Chicago's first settler (who was of African descent), this enthralling museum chronicles

Mosaic at the DuSable Museum of African American History

the African-American experience. There is a powerful exhibit on slavery, complete with shackles, while displays cover topics such as African hair art and the *Kwanzaa* holiday celebration *(see p101)*.

6 Ukrainian Institute of Modern Art

MAP B4 ▪ 2320 W. Chicago Ave. ▪ noon–4pm Wed–Sun ▪ www.uima-chicago.org

This tiny institute in the colorful Ukrainian Village neighborhood hosts rotating cultural programs, exhibitions, literary events, film screenings, and concerts. The permanent collection includes works by Chicago artists, as well as by painters and sculptors of Ukrainian descent.

Sculpture in Ukrainian Institute of Modern Art

7 International Museum of Surgical Science

MAP F4 ▪ 1524 N. Lake Shore Dr. ▪ 10am–4pm Tue–Fri, 10am–5pm Sat & Sun ▪ Adm (free Tue): $15; students and seniors $10, children (4–13) $7, members and under-3s free ▪ DA

Medicine meets the macabre at this museum, which displays historic instruments that span 4,000 years of surgery. Murals and sculptures pay tribute to the profession. Stronger stomachs may appreciate the ancient Peruvian skulls showing evidence of early surgical attempts.

8 Mary & Leigh Block Museum of Art

MAP B2 ▪ 40 Arts Circle Dr., Evanston ▪ 10am–5pm Tue, 10am–8pm Wed–Fri, 10am–5pm Sat & Sun

This collection of paintings, drawings, and sculpture is housed in a striking glass and limestone building designed by local architect Dirk Lohan. The museum offers rotating exhibitions, as well as numerous timely lectures and workshops.

9 Oriental Institute

In the heart of the University of Chicago campus, this museum showcases the work of University of Chicago researchers. It houses objects found in excavations in Egypt, Nubia, Persia, Mesopotamia, Syria, Anatolia, and ancient Megiddo. There are also temporary exhibitions *(see p102)*.

10 Jane Addams Hull House

Nobel Peace Prize-winning social reformer Jane Addams offered a brighter future to Chicago's immigrant population from these two Victorian houses. In addition to her original art and furniture, Hull House stages temporary exhibits relating to the social settlement that brought day care, counseling, and education to the working class *(see p97)*.

📐10 Parks and Beaches

1 Millennium and Grant Parks

As well as a center for world-class art, music, architecture, and landscape design, Millennium Park offers winter ice-skating, interactive public art, alfresco dining, and free classical music concerts and film screenings. Together with the adjoining 19th-century Grant Park, which hosts many festivals *(see pp66–7)*, it constitutes one of the finest, user-friendly green spaces in Chicago *(see p72)*.

2 North Avenue Beach

Chicago's most popular beach attracts a broad range of urban dwellers. Its lively ocean-liner-shaped bathhouse (including umbrella rentals, shower rooms, snack vendors, and a rooftop restaurant) makes it family friendly. Beach volleyball courts and a seasonal outdoor gym are a big draw *(see p89)*.

Kid's playground, Maggie Daley Park

Volleyball at North Avenue Beach

3 Oak Street Beach
MAP L1

At the foot of the chic Gold Coast shopping lane, this beach reflects its environs. Though just next to North Avenue Beach, you won't see many children here. Oak Street is usually filled with toned bodies and tiny bikinis. The crescent-shaped strand is the closest beach to the Magnificent Mile *(see pp32–3)* and makes a great place to stop and dip your toes after some serious shopping.

4 Maggie Daley Park

Maggie Daley Park marks the northeastern boundary of Grant Park. Named for the former first lady of Chicago, the park offers a range of diversions, including a seasonal ice-skating ribbon, climbing walls, and an elaborate playground for children. There are also tennis courts, picnic tables, and a garden dedicated to cancer survivors *(see p52)*.

5 Jackson Park
MAP F6

Laid out by the famed landscape designer Frederick Law Olmsted for the 1893 World's Columbian Exposition, Jackson Park, along with its Museum of Science and Industry *(see pp20–21)*, is among the few developments still remaining from that World's Fair. The South Side park includes a Japanese garden with waterfalls, colorful lanterns, and a bird sanctuary on an island in a peaceful lagoon.

6 Montrose Beach
MAP C3

Chicago's largest public beach is popular with families. Great for swimming, it has a changing house and shower facilities. Other activities include volleyball, sailboat and jet ski rentals, and a large number of trails for running and biking. The vast playing fields wedged between the sand and Lake Shore Drive are the domain of Hispanic soccer clubs: on weekends their numbers draw Latin food and balloon vendors. Kayak rentals launch here in summer.

7 Washington Square
MAP K2

Located opposite the historic Newberry Library, Washington Square is a prime plot of Gold Coast for resting tired feet and gazing at the handsome 1892 building. The park's ample benches tend to draw bookish sorts and picnicking office workers at lunchtime.

8 Lincoln Park
MAP F3

The greenway Lincoln Park stretches from North Avenue up to Hollywood Avenue, a recreational apron between lakefront and housing. In Chicago's infancy, the southern portion of the park was a cemetery for Civil War dead, which were later exhumed and interred elsewhere to make way for the park. Now Lincoln Park is the North Side's counterpart to Grant Park. Popular attractions such as Lincoln Park Zoo *(see pp30–31)*, the Lincoln Park Conservatory *(see p88)*, and Peggy Notebaert Nature Museum *(see p87)* supplement the beaches, harbors, playing fields, and bike paths.

South Pond Pavilion, Lincoln Park

9 Northerly Island
MAP M6

A peninsula jutting out in Lake Michigan south of the Alder Planetarium, Northerly Island is home to prairie plants, walking trails, and fountains. In summer it hosts concerts and special events at an outdoor stage that can accommodate 30,000 people on its lawn.

10 Ping Tom Memorial Park
MAP K6

Named in honor of a prominent Chinese businessman and civic leader, this rolling green space in Chinatown features Chinese design elements and public access to the river. A boat house offers kayak rentals in summer, and the field house hosts an indoor gym and swimming pool.

🔟 Film Locations

The Field Museum in *The Relic*

3 Field Museum
Scare-fest *The Relic* (1997) starred Penelope Ann Miller and Tom Sizemore as researchers trying to stop a murderous monster before it killed again. Many interior scenes were shot on replica sets but were near-perfect matches to the real museum *(see pp18–19)*.

4 Wrigley Field
The 1914-vintage Wrigley Field *(see p87)*, home to the Chicago Cubs, has starred in numerous baseball movies, including *The Natural*, *Rookie of the Year*, and *A League of Their Own*. It also has a cameo in *The Blues Brothers* and *Ferris Bueller's Day Off*.

5 Drake Hotel
In feel-good film *Hero* (1992), John Bubber (Andy Garcia) dupes the public into thinking he's a hero. Feeling guilty, he resolves to jump off a window ledge at The Drake *(see p117)*. Reality interrupted the filming when guests arrived for a party at the hotel. Director Stephen Frears protested and almost got arrested.

1 Michigan Avenue Bridge
In *Chain Reaction* (1996), Keanu Reeves is a science student at the University of Chicago *(see p101)* who is framed for murder. In a nail-biting chase scene, he trys to escape by running up the Michigan Avenue Bridge *(see p32)* as it's raised.

Michigan Avenue Bridge, featured in *Chain Reaction*

2 Daley Center and Plaza
Daley Plaza *(see p75)* was the setting for a chase scene in cult movie classic *The Blues Brothers* (1980). Stars John Belushi and Dan Aykroyd, playing ex-criminal brothers, dramatically crash their car through the center's plate-glass windows, specially installed for the filming.

A scene from *Hero* in the Drake Hotel

6 Palmer House Hilton

Wrongly accused and convicted of murder, Dr. Richard Kimble (Harrison Ford) dodges the authorities led by Tommy Lee Jones to prove his innocence in *The Fugitive* (1993). He winds up in a pulse-pounding chase through this grand hotel *(see p117)* onto its roof, down its elevator shaft, and into the hotel's laundry room.

7 Randolph "L" Station
MAP L4

The "L" tracks are an apt symbol of hard-working Chicago, and they feature significantly in the romantic comedy *While You Were Sleeping* (1995). Sandra Bullock plays an "L" station clerk who falls in love with a handsome commuter. He tumbles off the platform, Bullock saves his life, and comedy and romance ensue.

8 Wrigley Building

In *Road to Perdition* (2002) Tom Hanks is Michael Sullivan, an Irish gangster living in 1930s Chicago. After his wife and young son are murdered, he flees town with his older son. In seeking a safe refuge, they enter a hotel, the exterior of which is the beautiful Wrigley Building *(see p33)*. However, the interior scenes were actually filmed at the Palmer House Hilton.

9 The Art Institute of Chicago

The high-school comedy *Ferris Bueller's Day Off* (1986) stars Matthew Broderick, who skips school and takes his girlfriend (Mia Sara) and best friend (Alan Ruck) on an action-packed day. At the Art Institute, Broderick and Sara kiss in front of a window designed by Chagall, while Ruck stares intensely at *A Sunday on La Grande Jatte –1884 (see pp14–15)*.

Ferris at The Art Institute of Chicago

10 Union Station
MAP J4 ■ 210 S. Canal St.

Elliott Ness (Kevin Costner) brings down Chicago gangster Al Capone (Robert DeNiro) in the true story *The Untouchables* (1987). In one unforgettable scene, a shoot-out on a Union Station staircase causes a mother to lose her grip on her baby carriage, which bounces in slow motion down the stairs, saved at the last moment by Ness's partner.

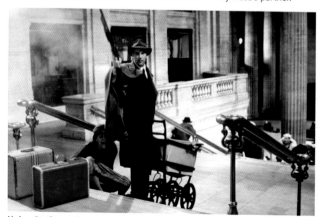

Union Station staircase sets the scene for *The Untouchables*

🔟 Off the Beaten Path

1 University of Chicago

Funded by oil magnate John D. Rockefeller (who deemed it his best ever investment), this forward-thinking institution opened in 1892 (see p101). The university campus is home to an attractive Neo-Gothic quad, the Oriental Institute (see p102), the Smart Museum of Art, the soaring Rockefeller Memorial Chapel, and Robie House (see p102).

2 Chicago Botanic Garden

MAP A1 ▪ 1000 Lake Cook Rd., Glencoe ▪ Metra station: Braeside ▪ 1-847-835-5440 ▪ Open 8am–sunset daily ▪ Adm ▪ DA ▪ www.chicago-botanic.org

North of Chicago are these natural and beautifully landscaped gardens. The most popular are the Rose Garden, the Japanese Garden, and the charming English Walled Garden.

3 Evanston

MAP B2 ▪ "L" station: Davis ▪ Visitors' Bureau: 1-847-448-4311

This suburb brims with restaurants, galleries, and shops. Northwestern University's Mary & Leigh Block Museum of Art (see p45) and Grosse Point Lighthouse are worth a visit.

The stunning Baha'i Temple

4 Baha'i Temple

MAP A1 ▪ 100 Linden Ave., Wilmette ▪ "L" station: Linden Ave. ▪ Visitors' Center open mid-May–mid-Sep 10am–8pm daily (to 5pm rest of the year); temple open 6am–10pm daily ▪ 1-847-853-2300 ▪ DA

This exquisite white structure is one of only eight temples of the Baha'i faith worldwide. Its nine doors symbolize how people can come to God from any direction. At night, spotlights enhance its ethereal beauty and intricate design.

5 Brookfield Zoo

MAP A6 ▪ 8400 W. 31st St., Brookfield ▪ Metra station: Hollywood ▪ CTA Bus: 331 ▪ 1-708-688-8000 ▪ Open 10am–5pm daily ▪ Adm (under-2s free) ▪ DA

Over 5,900 animals live together in themed, naturalistic environments at this popular zoo. Zones include Tropic World, where thunderstorms occur regularly (you stay dry) and Habitat Africa!, whose Forest exhibit has shy okapi and a re-created African village. In Be A Bird House, see what kind of bird you'd be on a machine that measures your flapping ability.

6 Bronzeville

MAP C5 ■ "L" station:
35th-Bronzeville-IIT (Green line)

A bronze memorial at Martin
Luther King, Jr. Drive and 35th
Street honors the journey many
African-Americans made to this
neighborhood as they fled the
oppression of the South in the early
20th century. Nearby, sidewalk
plaques celebrate local luminaries.
Bronzeville is Chicago's answer to
Harlem and offers jazz and blues
in its clubs, graceful mansions
aplenty, and lots of fine soul food.

7 Hemingway Birthplace

MAP A5 ■ "L" station: Oak Park
■ 1-708-524-5383 ■ Open 1–5pm
Sun–Fri, 10am–5pm Sat ■ Adm
■ www.ehfop.org

Oak Park (see pp36–7) is well known
as the first professional home of
architect Frank Lloyd Wright, and for
the concentration of Wright-designed
buildings he left behind. But Oak
Park was also home to a young
Ernest Hemingway; the author's
birthplace is open for tours.

8 Illinois Institute of Technology (IIT)

MAP C5 ■ 3300 S. Federal St. ■ "L"
station: 35th-Bronzeville-IIT (Green
line) ■ 312-567-3000 ■ Tours: www.
miessociety.org/home/tours ■ DA

In 1940, Ludwig Mies van der Rohe
planned the campus of this new
university. He also designed
around 20 of the buildings, which
demonstrate his design philosophies.
On arrival, stop by the on-campus
visitor center for information and
docent- or iPod-guided tours.

Illinois Institute of Technology

9 Garfield Park Conservatory

MAP B5 ■ 300 N. Central Park Ave.
■ "L" station: Conservatory-Central
Park Dr. (Green line) ■ 312-746-5100
■ Open 9am–5pm daily (to 8pm Wed)
■ DA ■ www.garfield-conservatory.org

Beneath glass-domed roofs, flora
from around the world thrives in
spacious greenhouses. Information
panels give the lowdown as you stroll
through six indoor areas that include
a Children's Garden and the Sweet
House (containing plants such as
cacao and sugar cane). Two grand
exhibition halls host special events.

Garfield Park Conservatory

10 Pullman National Monument

MAP B6 ■ Metra Station: Pullman/
111th St. ■ Visitors' Center: 11141 S.
Cottage Grove Ave., open 11am–3pm
Tue–Sun ■ 1-773-785-8901 ■ DA

Named a National Monument in 2015,
this industrial town was conceived in
the 1880s by railroad magnate George
Pullman for his workers. The planned
utopia had apartments, shops, a
hospital, and a hotel, but failed after
a strike in 1894, when a decrease in
wages made rents unaffordable.

🔟 Kids' Chicago

1 Emerald City Theatre Company

MAP D2 ▪ 2936 N. Southport Ave. ▪ 1-773-529-2690 ▪ Open Oct–May ▪ www.emeraldcitytheatre.com ▪ Adm

In Chicago there's a theater company for every demographic and Emerald City is its troupe devoted to young audiences. Expect lively productions such as *Where the Wild Things Are* as well as holiday-season shows in weekend-only midday matinees at Lincoln Park's Apollo Theater.

2 Maggie Daley Park

This 20-acre park *(see p75)*, tucked between Millennium Park and Lake Shore Drive, is a superb recreation area. The vast Play Garden for kids aged 12 and under has a pirate ship, swinging bridge, rope ladder, and Enchanted Forest with meandering paths and a rolling Wave Lawn. A seasonal ice ribbon makes a curvy path around the park's two rock climbing walls, which include routes for beginners (children must be able to wear the harnesses provided, which generally do not fit children under the age of 4), as well as for advanced climbers.

Display in Chicago Children's Museum

3 Chicago Children's Museum

MAP M3 ▪ 700 E. Grand Ave. ▪ 312-527-1000 ▪ Opening times vary ▪ Adm ▪ www.chicagochildrensmuseum.org

The engrossing, imaginative exhibits here emphasize doing – be it digging up a dinosaur bone or designing a water channel. A central, three-story rope tunnel immediately snares the attention of older visitors, though there are age-appropriate attractions for infants to pre-teens. If this place can't exhaust the younger set's energies, nowhere can.

4 Wrigley Field

A baseball-lover's park, Wrigley is a small and intimate stadium that's far less intimidating for children than many larger stadia *(see p87)*. A ticket to anywhere in the grandstand allows you to walk around and get to the rooftop terrace: the outfield stands can get rowdy, but a neighboring family section bans the beer that fuels the "bleacher bums."

5 Elevated Trains

Chicago's elevated trains (the "L") provide an inexpensive roofline tour of the city. The Brown Line in particular warrants a ride from Chicago Station over the Chicago River and around the Loop, threading between the massive buildings of the financial district *(see p108)*.

6 Chicago River Boat Tours

Even the smallest visitors will love a boat ride on the Chicago River, floating among the towering skyscrapers and listening to stories of the city and of how the river's flow was reversed to spare Lake Michigan its pollution. Wendella and Shoreline Sightseeing *(see p115)* both embark from Michigan Avenue, and offer family-friendly narration, from spring through to fall.

7 Lincoln Park Zoo

Free admission encourages repeat visits to the Lincoln Park Zoo *(see pp30–31)*. Many of the exhibits, including the working Farm in the Zoo and the Children's Zoo, allow kids to pet the animals. In summer, a motorized "train" makes a scenic loop around the park, while on the pond, swan-shaped paddleboats float among the ducks.

8 John G. Shedd Aquarium

Upon arrival, head straight for the Abbott Oceanarium to see the beluga whales and dolphins. Wild Reef re-creates a coral reef and houses sharks and other large predators. In the Polar Play Zone, kids can don a penguin suit and waddle in the Icy South play area or explore Arctic waters in the Icy North in a kids' size submarine. Children will also enjoy the special effects 4-D theater *(see pp28–9)*.

Dolphins at play, Shedd Aquarium

9 Museum of Science and Industry

Though this museum dazzles kids and adults alike with its submarine ship and replica coal mine, it's The Idea Factory that's designed just for juniors. With the pulling of gears and shifting of knobs, kids experiment through play with balance, construction, magnetism, and more. A current-fed waterway encourages boat building *(see pp20–23)*.

Maze, Museum of Science and Industry

10 Navy Pier

Kids make a beeline for Navy Pier's traditional carnival rides including a 196-ft- (60-m-) high ferris wheel and musical carousel. The ships that line the docks, from sleek, tall-masted schooners to powerful motorboats, will also grab their attention. All the restaurants here are family friendly *(see pp24–5)*.

🔟 Performing Arts

Inside the Civic Opera House

① Lyric Opera of Chicago

Established in 1954, the Lyric Opera is among the leading companies in the US, drawing top singers and directors. From September through May it offers a mix of classical operas, modern premieres, and popular musicals. Most are performed at the ornate Art Deco Civic Opera House, with its gleaming marble floors and crystal chandeliers (see p75).

② Court Theatre

MAP E5 ■ 5535 S. Ellis Ave.
■ www.courttheatre.org

This theater traces its roots to three Molière productions performed at the University of Chicago in 1955. The Court still mounts many classics, but it varies its seasons with musicals like *Guys and Dolls* and literary adaptations such as James Joyce's *The Dead*.

③ Chicago Symphony Orchestra

Conductor Riccardo Muti presides over the esteemed Chicago Symphony Orchestra and cellist Yo-Yo Ma is its creative consultant. The orchestra performs classical and contemporary pieces, with pop culture programs such as film scores thrown in. The orchestra's main home is the magnificent Symphony Center (see p75), but in summer they play at the outdoor suburban venue Ravinia.

④ Steppenwolf Theatre Co.

Founded in 1974 in a church basement, Steppenwolf has gained acclaim based on the fame of its ensemble, which includes actors John Malkovich and Gary Sinise. Though the company has moved to a specially built theater in Lincoln Park, it is still distinguished by raw emotion and edgy productions, and has received many notable accolades, including 12 Tony® Awards (see p88).

A performance at the Court Theatre

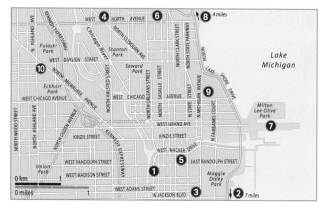

5 Goodman Theatre
MAP K3 ■ 170 N. Dearborn St.
■ www.goodmantheatre.org
One of Chicago's leading theater companies, the Goodman frequently spins off productions to Broadway in New York and has earned a Tony® Award. Noted productions include dramas by Eugene O'Neill and August Wilson and an annual version of Charles Dickens' *A Christmas Carol*.

6 Second City
MAP K2 ■ 1616 N. Wells St. ■ www.secondcity.com
Since 1959, Chicago's famed Second City comedy troupe has launched such comic lights as Tina Fey, Amy Poehler, and Bill Murray. Reservations are a must.

Facade detail, Second City

7 Chicago Shakespeare Theater
MAP M3 ■ 800 E. Grand Ave.
■ www.chicagoshakes.com
This Navy Pier venue presents a dynamic space for Shakespeare's repertory. The 510-seat courtyard design is inspired by the original layout in traditional playhouses of the Bard's day. Visiting non-Shakespeare productions take over after the company's September-to-April season.

8 Old Town School of Folk Music
MAP E3 ■ 4544 N. Lincoln Ave.
■ www.oldtownschool.org
Since the 1950s the Old Town School has brought world and homegrown folk music performers to Chicago. Its new home in Lincoln Square opened in 1998 with a concert by Joni Mitchell, though you're more likely to catch a women's ensemble from Mali and contemporary folkies.

9 Lookingglass Theatre
MAP L2 ■ 821 N. Michigan Ave.
■ www.lookingglasstheatre.org
In 1988, eight Northwestern University students founded Lookingglass, a bold company incorporating dance, circus arts, and live music in its original theatrical productions. Celebrity membership (including *Friends* actor David Schwimmer) and Broadway-bound shows have furthered this company's stardom.

10 House Theatre
MAP B4 ■ 1543 W. Division St.
■ www.thehousetheatre.com
Though it has moved out of storefronts and into the spacious Chopin Theater, this small troop epitomizes the creativity of Chicago theater. The group frequently writes its own works, which often cover epic themes and are popular with families.

TOP 10 Blues and Jazz Joints

Entrance to Rosa's

1 Rosa's
MAP E4 ▪ 3420 W. Armitage Ave. ▪ 1-773-342-0452 ▪ Closed Sun & Mon ▪ www.rosaslounge.com

Though off the beaten path, the family-owned Rosa's is beloved citywide for its support of local artists, such as blues harpist Sugar Blue, and for the genuine welcome extended by its owners, Tony Mangiullo and his mother Rosa. The latter sometimes cooks for the patrons of this simple tavern.

2 Kingston Mines
MAP E2 ▪ 2548 N. Halsted St. ▪ 1-773-477-4646 ▪ www.kingstonmines.com

The largest of Chicago's blues joints, Kingston Mines packs its Lincoln Park locale with students, young professionals, and a broader spectrum of tourists. Two stages provide non-stop musical entertainment from 8pm to near 4am (5am on Saturdays). Acts range from homegrown house bands to national touring headliners. The kitchen serves up beer-sopping, finger-licking barbecue food.

3 B.L.U.E.S.
MAP E2 ▪ 2519 N. Halsted St. ▪ 1-773-528-1012

Among Chicago's many blues clubs, B.L.U.E.S feels the most like a Southern juke joint. Chalk it up to the narrow confines, loud sounds, and sweaty dancers. The club is just across the street from the popular Kingston Mines, but it's a better choice for older, more musically versed blues fans. Better yet, why not stop into both!

4 House of Blues
MAP K3 ▪ 329 N. Dearborn St. ▪ 312-923-2000 ▪ www.houseofblues.com

Folk art and exotic architectural remnants festoon the funky House of Blues. The vast 1,500-seat concert hall presents a variety of national touring acts from hard rock to hip-hop in addition to blues. The Sunday gospel brunch with sittings from 9:30am to noon is a must.

5 Jazz Showcase
MAP K5 ▪ 806 S. Plymouth ▪ 312-360-0234 ▪ Open 8pm–2am Mon–Sat, 4pm–2am Sun ▪ www.jazzshowcase.com

A slick, reasonably priced jazz club that has been around since 1947, the Jazz Showcase offers some of the finest jazz in the city. Performances at this 170-seat venue are diverse, with professionals as well as bands from university music programs.

6 Andy's Jazz Club

MAP K3 ■ 11 E. Hubbard St.
■ 312-642-6805

With its musical program that begins at lunchtime and continues into the evening, Andy's fills a void for those jazz fans who can't hold out for the late-night headliners. Prime perches at the horseshoe-shaped bar are much sought after in this no-fuss River North club.

7 Green Mill Cocktail Lounge

MAP E2 ■ 4802 N. Broadway ■ 1-773-878-5552 ■ Limited DA

A former Prohibition-era speakeasy, Uptown's landmark Green Mill is a vintage treasure with a sweeping curved bar, vinyl booths, fading murals, and an authentic air of Chicago's gangster past. The city's premier jazz talents like Kurt Elling and Patricia Barber regularly play gigs here and Uptown Poetry Slam features every Sunday. It's out of the way but every cabbie in the city knows how to get there.

Buddy Guy headlining at his club

9 Buddy Guy's Legends

MAP L5 ■ 700 S. Wabash Ave.
■ 312-427-1190

A legend himself, bluesman Buddy Guy operates perhaps the best blues club in the city. The popular South Loop destination draws a mix of students, tourists, and local fans, particularly when Guy himself headlines (see p98).

10 California Clipper

1002 N. California Ave. ■ 1-773-384-2547 ■ www.californiaclipper.com

Home of the Purple Martini, this restored retro club, with a 40-ft (12-m) wooden bar and red-leather booths, bills itself as "the only bar with grape soda on its gun." Catch local, live country, dance, jazz, and blues from Thursday through Sunday (Monday is bingo night). See if you can spot "The Woman in White," the Clipper's elegant 1940s ghost.

Green Mill Cocktail Lounge

8 Blue Chicago

MAP K2 ■ 536 N. Clark St. & 736 N. Clark St. ■ 312-661-0100 ■ Open 8pm–1:30am Mon–Fri & Sun (to 2:30am Sat) ■ www.bluechicago.com

Popular with tourists, Blue Chicago in River North operates two clubs located two blocks apart. Seats at both venues are few and far between, so come early if you need one, or be prepared to dance. The admission charge covers both clubs, which encourages bar hopping.

Retro-style interior, California Clipper

🔟 Bars and Clubs

1 Cindy's

On the rooftop of the Chicago Athletic Association Hotel, the stylish, glass-roofed Cindy's feels like a garden party from opening hours to close. A terrace with two firepits offers panoramic views of Millennium and Grant parks, and Lake Michigan. Cocktail choices include large-format dispensers designed for sharing (see p77).

A night out at the Zebra Lounge

2 Zebra Lounge

An illegal speakeasy during Prohibition, this tiny piano bar has stood the test of time and competition, packing in loyal revelers nightly. Zebra prints dominate the decor, and martinis are the drink of choice. Singing along with the pianist to show tunes, torch songs, and oldies is expected (see p83).

3 Hideout

MAP D4 ▪ 1354 W. Wabansia Ave. ▪ 1-773-227-4433

Located off an industrial corridor on the Northside, Hideout is a popular destination for live music and arty performances. Many big names played here when they were rising stars, including Andrew Bird, and they often return. Events such as the Write Club pit debating scribes against one another.

4 Le Bar

MAP K2 ▪ 20 E. Chestnut St. ▪ 312-324-4000

In the beautiful Sofitel Hotel (see p116), a fashionable, over-30, mixed crowd fills this lobby lounge after work, lingering until the wee hours of the morning. Servers clad in black dispense martinis with scrumptious flavors such as chocolate and raspberry, and can cater to all tastes.

5 Sable Kitchen & Bar

MAP K3 ▪ 505 N. State St. ▪ 312-755-9704 ▪ Opening times vary

Named after Chicago's first non-native settler, Jean Baptiste Point du Sable (see p41), this dimly lit restaurant has a classic 1940s vibe to it. With its quintessential American dishes, interesting vegetarian options and an extensive appetizer list (which includes a range of delicious soups), Sable Kitchen & Bar is great for a lavish meal out.

6 The Violet Hour
MAP B4 ■ 1520 N. Damen Ave. ■ 1-773-252-1500

No sign marks the sophisticated Violet Hour in Wicker Park, a drape-swagged room that is Chicago's original artisan bar. Hostesses seat guests and waiting in line is common, but once ensconced in the exclusive high-backed chairs or booths, this is a great place to savor craft cocktails and lively conversation.

7 Billy Sunday
MAP B4 ■ 3143 W. Logan Blvd. ■ 1-773-661-2485

Chef Mathias Merges of nearby Yusho runs this upscale cocktail-focused bar located in Logan Square. If you're not familiar with bergamot bitters, Fernet or rhum agricole, it's best to quiz the creative mixologist. The bar also offers its own bottled and carbonated boozy sodas. A food menu of snacks and small plates keeps hunger pangs at bay.

8 Roof on the Wit
MAP K2 ■ 201 N. State St. ■ 312-239-9501 ■ Closed Sun

Nestled amid the skyscrapers of the Loop, with spectacular views of the city, the winding "L", the Chicago River, and Lake Michigan, the Wit is a chic complex of lounge bars.

Snuggle by an open fire and take in the ultra-hip ambience and stunning vistas, with a cocktail in hand.

9 Drumbar
MAP L2 ■ 201 E. Delaware Pl. ■ 312-943-5000 ■ Closed Sun & Mon

This stylish, contemporary rooftop bar offers great views of Chicago. An upscale nightclub with an innovative cocktail menu and a great wine list, Drumbar is a pricey yet classy establishment (dress code after 8pm).

Subterranean Three Dots and a Dash

10 Three Dots and a Dash
MAP K3 ■ 35 N. Clark St. ■ 312-610-4220

To find this hideaway, enter through the alley and descend to another time and place. Occupying several intimate rooms, this tiki bar includes a grass-thatch-fringed area serving pineapple-and-orchid-garnished drinks in classic tiki cups. Mai Tais and other cocktails pair well with *pupu platters* (island-style bar snacks).

Roof on the Wit, providing rooftop views over the city

🔟 Places to Eat

1 Girl & the Goat
MAP H4 ▪ 809 W. Randolph St. ▪ 312-492-6262 ▪ $$$

Popular chef Stephanie Izard is the girl in Girl & the Goat. Though she offers goat and other bold-flavored dishes, there is a particular emphasis on vegetables, which make up a third of the menu. Reserve a table well in advance, or chance your luck and arrive at opening time (4:30pm).

2 Alinea
Considered to be one of the world's foremost restaurants, Aliena has three Michelin stars and offers an exceptional gourmet experience. Chef Grant Achatz prepares tasting menus of highly creative New American dishes with wine or non-alcoholic pairings, served in three elegant dining areas with modern white and grey decor. The service is impeccable. Reserve well in advance (see p93).

3 Gibson's Steakhouse
MAP L2 ▪ 1028 N. Rush St. ▪ 312-266-8999 ▪ $$

Boisterous and convivial, Gibson's exudes a good time. A regular crowd of politicians, sports figures, and conventioneers packs the place nightly. The steakhouse fare is in every way a match to the atmosphere – big and bold. Huge lobster tails vie for attention with large slabs of beef. A reservation is critical, but for a more casual, walk-in experience try the burgers next door at Hugo's Frog Bar.

4 North Pond
Hidden from the road in leafy Lincoln Park, North Pond is a treasure – once you find it. Lodged in an Arts-and-Crafts-style building, the café offers an American seasonal menu with an emphasis on produce sourced in the Midwest.

Though dinner is the star, lunches of sandwiches, soups, and salads are equally creative and very well presented (see p93).

5 Spiaggia
Housed in an elegant tiered dining room, this upscale Italian restaurant has tables overlooking Oak Street Beach. It offers authentic, modern fare from award-winning chef Tony Mantuano, and a 700-bottle wine list. Café Spiaggia, its casual off-shoot at the same address, serves more rustic cuisine in relaxed yet stylish surroundings (see p83).

Spiaggia with floor-to-ceiling views

6 Blackbird
MAP J4 ▪ 619 W. Randolph St. ▪ 312-715-0708 ▪ Lunch 11:30am–2pm Mon–Fri, dinner 5–10pm Mon–Thu (to 11pm Fri & Sat) ▪ $$

Foodies and the fashion set both agree on Blackbird, a restaurant that sports minimalist decor and places the tables so close together that eavesdropping becomes part of the experience. Chef Paul Kahan generates the buzz, preparing sophisticated American dishes with French leanings. Menus change seasonally; reservations are essential.

Inventive fare, Blackbird

7 Next
MAP H3 ▪ 953 W. Fulton Market ▪ 312-226-0858 ▪ Closed Mon & Tue ▪ $$$

Founded by acclaimed chef Grant Achatz, Next reinvents itself each quarter with a new themed menu. Previous transformations include Paris Circa 1900, Childhood Memories, and Modern Chinese. Bookings are only sold through an advance ticketing system and sell out quickly, though resale options are often posted online.

8 Lou Mitchell's
MAP J4 ▪ 565 W. Jackson Blvd. ▪ 312-939-3111 ▪ No credit cards ▪ No dinner ▪ $

A classic diner in the Loop where the waitresses call you "Honey" and the coffee is bottomless, Lou Mitchell's has been around since 1923. Its trek-worthy meal is breakfast, highlighted by double-yolk eggs and homemade hash browns served in a skillet. Tables turn quickly and the staff doles out free donuts and candy with good cheer to those waiting in line.

9 Pizzeria Uno
MAP L3 ▪ 29 E. Ohio St. ▪ 312-321-1000 ▪ $

Uno's has been baking deep-dish pizza since 1943 – about as long as Chicagoans have debated whose pie is best. Its version comes several

Pizzeria Uno, a Chicago institution

inches deep, filled with cheese and toppings of your choice – truly a meal in one slice. The smallish Victorian brownstone strains under demand, sending the overflow up the street to its spin-off Pizzeria Due. Uno's individual pizza served at lunchtime is a real bargain.

10 Frontera Grill
Signature restaurant of chef Rick Bayless, Frontera Grill is credited with bringing authentic regional Mexican food – rather than Tex-Mex taco fare – stateside. Chili-roasted salsas and rich *moles* accompany grilled meats and delicious seafood. Since reservations are only available for parties of more than six, seats in the colorful, folk art-filled room go early as smaller groups try to avoid disappointment *(see p83)*.

🔟 Shopping Destinations

1 State Street

A slew of chain stores line this legendary street (see p73), but it's the two old-time department stores that make it unique. The former Marshall Field's, now Macy's (see p76), here since 1907, has merchandise to satisfy every wealthy shopper's needs. At TJ Maxx the prices are lower, but the variety is still extensive (see p76).

Inside Macy's, State Street

2 Oak Street

MAP L1 ■ Borders: N. Michigan Ave. & Rush St.

If you have to ask how much it costs, you should probably plan on just window-shopping along this stretch of Chicago's upper-crust Gold Coast. Boutiques here sell designer wear, accessories, and shoes fit for a Paris runway – and include some shops exclusive to Chicago such as Tessuti (menswear) and Designs by Ming (custom clothing design).

3 Andersonville

MAP B3 ■ Clark St. between Foster and Bryn Mawr

This far Northside neighborhood hosts a string of independent boutiques along bustling Clark Street. Zoning regulations have kept out big-box stores with the result that the bookshops, galleries, design stores, and clothing specialists offer unique goods.

4 Bucktown Neighborhood

MAP B4 ■ Borders: Fullerton Ave. to Division Ave. & Kennedy Expressway to Western Ave.

Once a hotspot for starving artists, Bucktown and adjacent Wicker Park are now gentrified locales brimming with vintage clothes stores, edgy music shops, high-style designer boutiques, and antiques importers.

5 Bloomingdale's Home and Furniture Store

MAP K3 ■ 600 N. Wabash Ave. ■ Opening times vary ■ DA

This store's lovingly restored 1913 Moorish-style building is an attraction in its own right. Inside there's a sleek, four-level atrium with home decor departments that sell everything from bedding to furniture.

6 Broadway Antique Market

MAP E2 ■ 6130 N. Broadway ■ Open 11am–7pm, Mon–Sat, 11am–6pm Sun ■ DA

An old-time movie palace sign indicates the 1939 building that houses this market. With 85 dealers stocking artwork, jewelry, clothing, and more in styles such as Arts and Crafts, Art Deco, and Mid-Century Modern, you're sure to find something to suit.

Broadway Antique Market

Magnificent Mile
This stretch of North Michigan Avenue is one of the world's retail meccas. Besides sophisticated designer boutiques, there are malls (each with high-end department stores); and big-name chain and flagship stores (see pp32–3).

Retail heaven, Magnificent Mile

 Architectural Artifacts
MAP B3 ▪ 4325 N. Ravenswood Ave. ▪ Open 10am–5pm daily
This sprawling warehouse on the Northside is chock-full of architectural and antique cast-offs, many from demolished buildings. Wares come from Chicago, Europe, and South America and range from massive stone mantles to neon signs and ceramic art tiles.

 CAF Shop
MAP L6 ▪ 224 S. Michigan Ave. ▪ Open 9:30am–6:30pm Mon–Thu, 9am–7pm Fri, 9am–6:30pm Sat & Sun ▪ DA
The CAF (Chicago Architecture Foundation) Shop, located in the historic Santa Fe Center (see p74), is part of the CAF's ArchiCenter, which also puts on exhibitions and runs city tours. Browse the shop for architecture and design-related books; art-glass panels and lamps in Frank Lloyd Wright designs; desk gadgets; and desirable kitchen gizmos.

Armitage Avenue
This tree-lined street in Lincoln Park (see p47) is a favorite for those who are seeking out-of-the-ordinary clothing, home decor, bath and body products – and don't mind spending more to get it.

TOP 10 CHICAGO SOUVENIRS

1 Frango Mints
Marshall Field's/Macy's (see p76) doesn't make these delicious mint chocolates anymore, but still sells them by the box-full.

2 Blues & Jazz CDs
CDs by Chicago music legends are on sale at the Water Works Visitor Information Center (see p80).

3 Vosges Haut Chocolat
The Chicago-based Vosges Haut Chocolat makes exotic velvety truffles with global flavors.

4 Art Poster
See the real thing, then buy a copy at the extensive Art Institute of Chicago gift shop (see p14).

5 Sports Jersey
Clubs T-shirts, Blackhawks sweaters, and Bulls jerseys make very popular apparel purchases.

6 Cubs Baseball Cap
Head to the Tribune Tower (see p80) gift shop for caps of the Major League team owned by the Chicago Tribune.

7 Art Glass
Take home a little Prairie style with a replica Frank Lloyd Wright art-glass panel from the CAF (Chicago Architecture Foundation) store.

8 Garrett's Popcorn
Garrett's Popcorn, especially the signature cheddar-caramel mix, is a classic Chicago guilty pleasure.

9 Sue Skeleton
Sue, the world's largest T. rex skeleton is far less menacing in mini model form from the Field Museum (see p18).

10 Chicago Snowglobe
Recall Chicago winters with a city skyline snowglobe from Accent Chicago in the Water Tower Place mall (see p32).

Chicago Blackhawks jersey

🔟 Chicago for Free

① Navy Pier
Navy Pier offers some of the best and most scenic strolling in the city. The pier is carnival-like, with myriad attractions begging you to spend money, but entry itself is free, as are the Wednesday and Saturday night firework displays in summer (see pp24–5).

② Lincoln Park Zoo
Lincoln Park Zoo is one of the last free zoos in the country. There is no admission charge to see the apes, polar bears, birds, and more unusual animals. Daily sea lion feedings at 2pm are a great show (see pp30–31).

③ Public Art
Many famous artists, such as Pablo Picasso, Alexander Calder, and Marc Chagall have left their artistic mark on the city. Details of public art downtown are included in the Loop Sculpture Guide, downloadable from www.cityofchicago.org.

④ Lakefront Recreational Path
The 18-mile (29-km) paved path that runs along Lake Michigan is popular for running, cycling, skating, and walking. Many hotels offer rental bicycles and the city's bike-share program Divvy (see side bar) offers cheap wheels.

Blues festival for free at Grant Park

⑤ Free Events
Mayor's Office of Special Events (recorded info): 312-744-3370 ■ www. cityofchicago.org/specialevents
Summer in Chicago brings lots of free outdoor festivals, from the big music events of Grant Park, such as the Chicago Blues Festival (see p66), to parades, circuses in the parks, and neighborhood festivals that feature entertainment and vendors.

⑥ Comedy Shows
Comedy Sportz: 929 W. Belmont St.; 1-773-549-8080; www.comedysportzchicago.com ■ iO Theater: 3541 N. Clark St.; 1-773-880-0199; www.ioimprov.com/chicago
Chicago is the place to catch the best rising comedy and improv stars. The iO Theater runs dozens of shows each week from its Lincoln Park

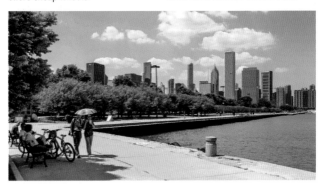
Lakefront Recreational Path, great for strolling or cycling

headquarters, some of them free and all of them a blast. Also check Comedy Sportz for freebies.

7 Brewery Tours

Lagunitas Brewing: 2607 W. 17th St.; 1-773-522-2097; www. lagunitas.com ■ Revolution Brewing: 2323 N. Milwaukee Ave.; 1-773-227-2739; www.revbrew.com

Several microbreweries offer free tours of their facilities, including the sprawling Lagunitas Brewing in Pilsen. Tours begin in a recreation room with generous free samples, pinball machines, and other old-time amusements. Revolution Brewing in Logan Square also offers guided tours Wednesday to Sunday.

8 Free Museums

Seek out the smaller museums that offer free admission, including the National Museum of Mexican Art *(see p44)*.

Millennium Park drawing a crowd

9 Millennium Park Programming

Over the summer, Millennium Park *(see pp34–5)* hosts a series of free events and performances, ranging from concerts by the Lyric Opera *(see p54)* and Chicago Children's Choir to screenings of popular movies.

10 Free Tours

The tourism bureau Choose Chicago *(see p113)* offers free guided tours led by locals. Sign up 10 days in advance via the website for a Chicago Greeter tour running for 2 to 4 hours. Or if you haven't planned ahead, InstaGreeters are available for 1-hour tours Friday to Sunday *(see p114)*.

TOP 10 MONEY-SAVING TIPS

Chicago's popular Divvy bikes

1 Purchase half-price tickets for same-day theater performances at three Hot Tix booths. See www.hottix.org for shows available.

2 Many restaurants have good-value "Early Bird Specials" or pre-theater menus. Look for signs throughout the city advertising these deals.

3 Chicago's many beautiful parks offer free skating rinks, beaches, pools, tennis courts, and lots of walking and cycling paths.

4 Choose Chicago offers several promotions, such as Winter Delights, which include discounts on lodging, attractions, and meals; www. choosechicago.com.

5 CityPass grants entry to five top attractions including the Shedd Aquarium and Field Museum for 50 percent off; www.citypass.com.

6 Take unlimited 30-minute rides with one of the city's Divvy bikes. A day pass costs $9.95; www.divvybikes.com.

7 Ring the Loop aboard the Brown Line "L" running out to Lincoln Park and back again for a scenic tour at just $2.25 *(see pp108–9)*.

8 Look for neighborhood restaurants that lack a liquor license and allow diners to bring their own beer or wine.

9 Skip the observatory at the John Hancock Center *(see p79)* and hit its 95th-floor Signature Lounge for equivalent views.

10 Visit the Chicago Cultural Center to see its stained-glass domes and to catch some of the free concerts that are regularly scheduled here *(see p71)*.

TOP 10 Festivals and Events

1 Chicago Blues Festival
MAP L6 ▪ Late May–early Jun

The raucous weekend-long Blues Festival kicks off summer in Chicago. An estimated 750,000 listeners converge on Grant Park for the world's largest free blues event. The main stage hosts traditional bluesmen like Honeyboy Edwards, jazz interpreters such as Mose Allison, and blues-inflected artists like Bonnie Raitt. Smaller side stages offer a more intimate experience.

2 Lollapalooza
MAP L6 ▪ Late July
▪ www.lollapalooza.com

The three-day rock festival known as Lollapalooza takes over Grant Park in late July. Major headliners such as Paul McCartney and Florence + the Machine are joined by emerging rockers, DJs, and techno innovators spread over several stages across the park. Passes go on sale, and usually sell out, in March.

3 Chicago Air and Water Show
312-744-3316 ▪ Mid-Aug

This display of military power features historic aircraft flybys, a staged amphibious attack, and precision flying teams. Prime viewing spots are from Oak Street to Montrose Beach.

Chicago Air and Water Show

Chicago Jazz Festival

4 Chicago Jazz Festival
MAP L6 ▪ 312-744-3316 ▪ Late Aug/early Sep (inc. Labor Day weekend)

The Jazz Fest caps summer, when music fans are drawn to Grant Park for free concerts by greats like Branford Marsalis and Roy Hargrove.

5 Chicago Gospel Music Festival
MAP L6 ▪ 312-744-3316 ▪ Early Jun
▪ www.choosechicago.com

For three days Grant Park resounds with stirring choirs and impassioned soloists. Headliners have included soul singer Al Green.

6 World Music Festival
312-744-3315 ▪ Mid-Sep
▪ www.worldmusicfestivalchicago.org

This city-wide, multi-venue, week-long festival showcases the very best of traditional and contemporary international music. Concerts are low-cost or even free.

7 Magnificent Mile Holiday Lights Festival

MAP L2 ▪ Mid-Nov–end Dec

Merchants mark the start of the holiday season by lighting the shops, lampposts, and trees along Michigan Avenue. The parade and fireworks above the Chicago River on the Saturday night before Thanksgiving warrant braving the inevitable chill.

8 Taste of Chicago

MAP L6 ▪ Grant Park
▪ 312-744-3316 ▪ Late Jun–early Jul

Chicago's signature foods star during the nearly two-week-long Taste of Chicago. Musical entertainers, a carnival with rides, and cooking demonstrations entertain at the sprawling Grant Park event.

Entrance to Taste of Chicago

9 Old Town Art Fair

MAP F4 ▪ 1763 N. Park Ave.
▪ 312-337-1938 ▪ Jun ▪ Adm
▪ www.oldtownartfair.org

This 50-year-old fair installs 250 artist booths along Old Town's lanes. There are also food vendors, kids' entertainment, and garden tours.

10 Chicago Summer Neighborhood Festivals

312-744-3316 ▪ May–Sep
▪ www.choosechicago.com

Chicago has upwards of 100 neighborhood festivals. Virtually every summer weekend features an event or three, ranging from the gay-oriented North Halsted Market Days to the ethnic Korean Street Festival.

TOP 10 SPORTS TEAMS AND EVENTS

Chicago Bears in action

1 Chicago Cubs
Despite the Cubbies' losing streak, their baseball games at the Wrigley Field are often sell-outs (see p87).

2 Chicago White Sox
Apr–Sep ▪ www.whitesox.com
The White Sox are renowned for their top-quality baseball.

3 Chicago Bears
Sep–Dec ▪ www.chicagobears.com
The football team generates rabid fans and tailgate picnics when in action on Soldier Field (see p12).

4 Chicago Bulls
Oct–Apr ▪ www.bulls.com
Their basketball hasn't been the same since superstar Michael Jordan left.

5 Chicago Blackhawks
Oct–Apr ▪ www.chicago
blackhawks.com
NHL ice hockey team sharing the United Center (see p13) with the Bulls.

6 Arlington Park
May–Sep ▪ www.arlingtonpark.com
Thoroughbred horses race at this park just north of Chicago.

7 Chicago Fire
Apr–Oct ▪ www.chicago-fire.com
Many local Latino soccer fans support the Fire.

8 Chicago Wolves
Oct–May ▪ www.chicagowolves.com
Four-time league champions offer a great evening of hockey.

9 Chicago Marathon
Oct ▪ www.chicagomarathon.com
40,000 entrants run through the city.

10 Chicago Triathlon
Aug ▪ www.chicagotriathlon.com
Over 6,000 run, bike, and swim in this action-packed one-dayer.

Chicago
Area by Area

Chicago's Gold Coast area fringed by Oak Street Beach

The Loop	**70**
Near North	**78**
Northside	**86**
South Loop	**94**
Far South	**100**

TOP10 The Loop

Named for the ring of elevated train tracks that encircle it, this is downtown Chicago's core, and the city's financial and governmental hub. Abuzz with laptop-toting business folk during the week, the Loop is transformed on weekends when a veritable shopping frenzy erupts along its famous State Street. Those thirsty for culture come flocking to see the collections of the Art Institute of Chicago and to view the area's many architecturally significant buildings and its notable public art, while public parks offer green recreational spaces and the Riverwalk pedestrian path is a great place for strolling. The theater district, with its variety of shows, and the many great bars and restaurants give the area a lively nightlife.

Lion statue, the Art Institute of Chicago

AREA MAP OF THE LOOP

The Best of the Rest

1 **Loop Theater District**
MAP K4

A sidewalk plaque at Randolph and State streets denotes Chicago's officially designated Theater District, a cluster of old and new theaters.

2 **Civic Opera House**
MAP J4 ■ 20 N. Wacker Dr.
■ www.lyricopera.org

This 1929 structure was inspired by Paris's Opera Garnier. It is home to the Lyric Opera of Chicago *(see p54)*.

3 **Old St. Patrick's Church**
MAP J4 ■ 700 W. Adams St.

Chicago's oldest church (1856) is crowned by two towers – one Romanesque, one Byzantine – symbolizing East and West.

4 **Maggie Daley Park**
MAP L4 ■ 37 E. Randolph St.

If Millennium Park is about art, its neighbor just to the east is all about play. Features include an elaborate children's playground, two climbing walls, tennis courts, and a popular frozen skating ribbon in winter.

5 **Symphony Center**
MAP L4 ■ 220 S. Michigan Ave.
■ www.cso.org

At the heart of this center is Orchestra Hall (1904), the stunning home of the Chicago Symphony Orchestra *(see p54)*.

Orchestra playing, Symphony Center

6 **Chicago Temple**
MAP J4 ■ 77 W. Washington St.

A Gothic-inspired structure designed by Holabird and Roche in 1923. Under the majestic spire is a 35-seat chapel.

7 **Federal Reserve Bank**
MAP K4 ■ 230 S. LaSalle St.

This impressive edifice is one of 12 regional Reserve banks. When it was first built in 1922, it had the largest bank vaults ever constructed.

The logo of Chicago's Foodseum

8 **Foodseum Chicago**
MAP K3 ■ 19 N. Dearborn St.
■ www.foodseum.org

This museum presents rotating exhibits devoted to food, often with a local bent, such as hot dogs and Chicago's role in popularizing them.

9 **Palmer House Hilton**

The first Palmer House was destroyed in the Great Chicago Fire *(see p40)*. The current hotel is lavish, decorated with frescos, Tiffany light fixtures, and marble floors *(see p117)*.

10 **Daley Plaza**
MAP K4

Home to the county court head-quarters, Daley Plaza is best known for its unnamed giant steel Picasso sculpture (1967) donated by the artist.

Shops

View from the upper floors, Macy's

1 Macy's
MAP K4 ▪ 111 N. State St. ▪ DA

Once Marshall Field's, Chicago's oldest and best-known department store is famous for its elaborate Christmas displays, dazzling Tiffany dome, and iconic clock. Established more than 100 years ago, it offers top clothing and homeware *(see p62)*.

2 TJ Maxx
MAP K4 ▪ 11 N. State St. ▪ DA

This department store offers a wide variety of clothing for adults and children. A great place to find quality brands at the cheapest prices.

3 Block 37
MAP K4 ▪ 108 N. State St. ▪ DA

The Loop's answer to the malls of the Magnificent Mile contains brands such as Sephora and Zara. Its Latin food hall is popular at lunch.

4 H&M
MAP K4 ▪ 22 N. State St. ▪ DA

This bargain store offers trendy clothes for all occasions, including a collection especially suited for teenagers and under-30s.

5 Old Navy
MAP K4 ▪ 150 N. State St. ▪ DA

This regional flagship store offers the ultimate Old Navy shopping experience, with two floors of discount jeans and T-shirts, and other casual comfort clothes.

6 Jewelers Center
MAP K4 ▪ 5 S. Wabash Ave. ▪ Closed Sun ▪ DA

On the strip commonly known as "Jewelers Row" this 1912 Art Deco building contains over 180 jewelers. It is a friendly place to shop for gold, pearls, watches, diamonds, and gems at relatively low prices.

7 Nordstrom Rack
MAP K4 ▪ 24 N. State St.

High style on sale at a fraction of the original prices lures bargain hunters to this charming little sister of the upscale and pricey Nordstrom.

8 Blick Art Materials
MAP K4 ▪ 42 S. State St. ▪ DA

This two-story family-owned store carries a wide range of cards, stationery and arty gifts in addition to its massive stock of fine art supplies.

9 Gallery 37 Store
MAP L4 ▪ 66 E. Randolph St. ▪ DA

Teenage artists involved in an arts training program create the incredible paintings, sculptures, and other artwork sold here. All proceeds from sales are returned to the program.

10 Iwan Ries & Co.
MAP L4 ▪ 19 S. Wabash Ave. ▪ Closed Sun ▪ DA

Trading since 1857, this store sells a vast selection of cigars, pipes, and smoking accessories.

Places to Eat and Drink

PRICE CATEGORIES
Price categories include a three-course meal for one, a glass of house wine, tax, and a 15–20 percent tip.

....

$ under $30 $$ $30–$60 $$$ over $60

1 Everest
MAP K5 ■ 440 S. LaSalle St.
■ 312-663-8920 ■ Closed lunch, Sun & Mon ■ $$$

The restaurant on the top floor of the Chicago Stock Exchange has spectacular views and chocolate soufflé to die for.

2 The Gage
MAP L4 ■ 24 S. Michigan Ave.
■ 312-372-4243 ■ $$

Across from Millennium Park, this popular restaurant occupies a series of 19th-century millinery shops and has a vaguely Irish concept, serving Guinness on draft. The extensive menu highlights contemporary seasonal dishes.

3 Park Grill
MAP L4 ■ 11 N. Michigan Ave.
■ 312-521-7275 ■ $$

The only restaurant in Millennium Park, Park Grill would still be crowded even if it didn't try so hard. Its cooking, from burgers to salads and salmon *au poivre*, is superior.

4 Cherry Circle Room
MAP L4 ■ 12 S. Michigan Ave.
■ 312-792-3515 ■ $$

The restaurant in the Chicago Athletic Club offers intimate booths and antique furnishings. The equally stylish menu riffs on retro dishes, but with a creative modern twist and fresh seasonal produce.

5 Acanto
MAP L4 ■ 18 S. Michigan Ave.
■ 312-578-0763 ■ $$

From the owners of the neighboring Gage, Acanto, near Millennium Park, offers authentic Italian specialties from salumi to duck-egg spaghetti.

6 Petterinos
MAP K4 ■ 150 Dearborn St.
■ 312-422-0150 ■ $$

This pre- and post-theater Loop restaurant looks like an old-school supper club with its jacketed waiters, but it operates with modern efficiency. Good pastas and chops are on the menu, and the bar is a popular post-curtain haunt for actors.

Chic decor and great views at Cindy's

7 Atwood Café
MAP K4 ■ Hotel Burnham, 1 W. Washington St. ■ 312-368-1900 ■ $$

Expect top-notch hotel dining, where creative American cuisine leans toward comfort food.

8 Cindy's
MAP L4 ■ 12 S. Michigan Ave.
■ 312-792-3502 ■ $$

Crowds flock to rooftop Cindy's for the views over Millennium Park. Its menu caters to a convivial crowd, with sharable dishes such as seafood platters served at wooden picnic-inspired tables.

9 Russian Tea Time
MAP L4 ■ 77 E. Adams St.
■ 312-360-0000 ■ $$

A spirited taste of Russia, where the vodka flows freely and the beef stroganoff is a crowd-pleaser.

10 Terzo Piano
MAP L4 ■ 159 E. Monroe Dr.
■ 312-443-8650 ■ $

Located on the third floor of the Art Institute, Terzo Piano serves satisfying Italian café fare from chef Tony Mantuano of Spiaggia.

See map on pp70–71

🔟 Near North

History, culture, and commerce collide on Chicago's densely packed Near North side. This area is a pleasure to explore on foot, whether you are interested in shopping or fine art and architecture. The city's classiest shopping boulevard – the Magnificent Mile – bridges the posh 19th-century mansions of the lakeside Gold Coast (which has its own clutch of upscale boutiques) and the former industrial warehouses of River North, now mostly converted into art galleries. In addition to these, there are two local art museums. But ultimately, it's the Magnificent Mile on a Saturday that says more about Midwestern vitality and giddy American consumerism than any other Chicago experience.

AREA MAP OF NEAR NORTH

❶ Top 10 Sights
see pp79–81

① Places to Eat and Drink
see p83

① Shopping
see p82

1 John Hancock Center

MAP L2 ■ 875 N. Michigan Ave.
■ Observatory open 9am–11pm daily,
Adm., DA ■ Signature Room open
daily, DA ■ www.johnhancock
centerchicago.com

Skidmore, Owings & Merrill
designed this 1970 landmark using
the signature Xs on the facade as
cross-braces to help the 1,100-ft
(335-m) building withstand the winds
coming off Lake Michigan. Soak up
the view from the 94th-floor
observation deck or drink it in from
the Signature Room restaurant and
lounge directly above. Many say you
get a better view from here than
from the South Side's Sears Tower –
and the lines are usually shorter too.

2 Merchandise Mart

MAP K3 ■ 222 W. Merchandise
Mart Plaza ■ DA

This massive two-square-block
edifice houses Chicago's premier
interior design trade showrooms.
When completed in 1930, the four
million-sq-ft (390,000-sq-m) building
was the largest in the world. Today, it
is second only to the Pentagon in
size, and is still the world's largest
commercial building. The Chicago
Architecture Foundation (see p63)
offers a 45-minute guided tour, which
is a great way to get to grips with this
daunting building.

Magnificent – or Mag – Mile

3 Magnificent Mile

Whether you're a shopper or
not, this store-lined strip warrants
a visit if only to get a feel for the
commercial pulse that seems to
keep Chicago humming (see pp32–3).

4 Museum of Contemporary Art

MAP L2 ■ 220 E. Chicago Ave. ■ Open
Tue–Sun 10am–5pm (to 8pm Tue)
■ Adm (free on Tue) ■ DA
■ www.mcachicago.org

One of the country's largest collections
of international contemporary art,
the MCA has over 6,000 objects, from
painting and sculpture to photography
and video installations. In summer,
the sculpture garden and displays of
performance art on the front lawn
enhance the experience.

The impressive stairwell, Museum of Contemporary Art

Aerial view, Gold Coast Area

the newspaper whose offices still occupy the building. Look closely at the facade, which is embedded with over 120 stones collected by correspondents from famed sights. There's a rock hailing from each of the 50 states, as well as fragments from international monuments such as Greece's Parthenon, India's Taj Mahal, and The Great Wall of China.

5 Gold Coast Area
MAP K1

Chicago boasts many upscale neighborhoods, but none more historic and prestigious than the Gold Coast. Railroad, retail, and lumber tycoons built this elegant district in the decades following the Great Fire of 1871 (see p40), and its leafy streets are lined with 19th-century mansions interspersed with early 20th-century apartment buildings. There are no fewer than 300 designated historic landmarks in the Astor Street District alone, including buildings by Stanford White (such as 20 E. Burton Place), and Charnley House (1365 N. Astor Street), designed by Louis Sullivan (assisted at the time by Frank Lloyd Wright).

6 Tribune Tower
MAP L3 ■ **435 N Michigan Ave.**

Topped by flying buttresses, this Gothic-style building was completed in 1925. Its faux-historic design had won a competition organized by Colonel Robert McCormick, publisher of the *Chicago Tribune*,

7 River North Gallery District
MAP K3 ■ **Bounded by Merchandise Mart (south), Chicago Ave. (north), Orleans Ave. (west), Dearborn St. (east)** ■ **Chicago Gallery News: 312-649-0064; www.chicagogallerynews.com**

Said to be the most concentrated art hub in the US outside of Manhattan, this district is jammed with galleries. Most are found in the handsome, 19th-century converted brick warehouses found alongside the "L" brown line. Huron and Superior streets are particularly worth a visit.

8 Chicago Water Works and Pumping Station
MAP L2 ■ **Water Works and Pumping Station: 163 E. Pearson St. & 806 N. Michigan Ave.** ■ **Visitor Center: open 7:30am–7pm Mon–Thu; 312-337-0665; www.choosechicago.com** ■ **City Gallery: open 10am–6:30pm daily; 312-742-0808; DA**

When the Great Fire of 1871 swept north, only the 1869 Water Works and Pumping Station escaped. Built by William W. Botington, the castellated Gothic-Revival Water Works was modeled after a medieval castle. It now houses the Chicago Visitor Center and the Lookingglass Theatre (see p55), and the fountain and chairs outside make it a focal point for street life. The functioning Pumping Station across the street houses the City Gallery, which specializes in photography.

Chicago Water Works

9 Fourth Presbyterian Church

MAP L2 ■ 126 E. Chestnut St.
■ Open 9am–5pm Mon–Sat,
7am–5pm Sun ■ DA

The first Fourth Presbyterian church, dedicated in 1871, celebrated its first sermon just hours before it was incinerated in the Great Fire. Rebuilt in 1914, today's church offers a peaceful respite from Magnificent Mile. Designed by Ralph Adams Cram, one of the architects behind New York's Cathedral of St. John the Divine, this church has a cathedral-like interior, with a splendid stained-glass west window. Free concerts take place on Fridays at noon.

Interior, Fourth Presbyterian Church

10 Newberry Library

MAP K2 ■ 60 W. Walton St.
■ 312-943-9090 ■ Open 9am–5pm
Mon–Fri (to 1pm Sat)

Founded in 1887 by wealthy Chicago businessman Walter L. Newberry, this research library is housed in a Romanesque-style granite building designed by architect Henry Ives Cob. It is stocked with rare books, maps, manuscripts, and music, and has research centers devoted to the history of cartography, American Indian and Indigenous studies, the Renaissance, and American history and culture. It also offers seminars on everything from Greek literature to genealogy research. The public can use the collections by applying for a reader's card free of charge.

A DAY IN THE NEAR NORTH

▶ MORNING

Line up early with the locals for a fortifying stack at **The Original Pancake House** (22 E. Bellevue Pl.). Afterward, stroll south on Rush Street to Oak Street. Take a left and walk the most exclusive shopping block in the city, where you can pop into stores such as Barneys New York. Once you hit Michigan Avenue, it's a short jaunt to the **John Hancock Center** (see p79) for sky-high views. Back on terra firma, cross the street to the **Chicago Water Works** for a close-up look at a piece of Chicago's history. Lovers of modern art should cross Michigan again and head to the **Museum of Contemporary Art** (see p79).

AFTERNOON

Everyone will get what they want for lunch at Foodlife, a food court on the second level of the mall in **Water Tower Place** (see p32). You can shop the seven floors of Chicago's first ever vertical mall, and then shop some more – and sightsee – along the **Magnificent Mile** (see pp32–3). If you've worked up an appetite, stroll over to **The Drake** hotel (see p117) for high tea, which is served until 5pm.

EVENING

Catch a show at Lookingglass Theatre, housed in the **Water Works Pumping Station**. Then head to chic NoMI in the Park Hyatt Chicago (see p83) for dinner and drinks with panoramic views of the landmark Water Tower and downtown Chicago.

See map on p78 ←

Shopping

1 Burton
MAP L2 ▪ 56 E. Walton St.
You don't have to be a snow boarder to shop at this flagship store, known for its range of funky boards and bold cold-weather gear.

2 Barneys New York
MAP L1 ▪ 15 E. Oak St.
This branch of the Big Apple's downtown department store draws together the latest cosmetics, shoes, jewelry, accessories, and men's and women's apparel in a minimalist, open-plan, tri-level space.

3 American Girl Place
MAP L2 ▪ Water Tower Place, 835 N. Michigan Ave.
▪ 1-877-247-5223
Parents of girls aged four to twelve make a beeline for this store, the only retail outlet of the American Girl line of dolls. A theater and café supplement three floors devoted to dolls, books, and other accessories.

American Girl Place

4 Ikram
MAP L2 ▪ 873 N. Rush St.
Launched by a former Ultimo buyer, Ikram specializes in high-end women's fashion sold at top dollar. Chic wares and lines change seasonally, but shop assistance is uniformly personal.

5 Polo Ralph Lauren
MAP L2 ▪ 750 N. Michigan Ave.
This massive four-story shop is so successful at transforming itself from a store to a den devoted to Ralph Lauren's to-the-manor-born lifestyle – note the horse and hound paintings throughout – that it warrants a visit from even the less well-heeled among us.

6 Anthropologie
MAP K2 ▪ 111 E. Chicago Ave.
Women's apparel with a bohemian bent and housewares gathered from around the world sell briskly at this large, loft-like store.

7 P.O.S.H.
MAP K3 ▪ 613 N. State St.
Recalling the days of elegant steamships and grand hotels, this store uses old-fashioned suitcases and steamer trunks to lovingly display vintage china and silverware engraved with hotel and ship logos.

8 Paper Source
MAP J2 ▪ 232 W. Chicago Ave.
This arty River North shop is part art supply store, part stationer. The creative selection of cards and small gifts includes handmade stationery, cloth-covered sketchbooks, and novel desktop accessories.

9 Original Penguin
MAP L2 ▪ 901 N. Rush St.
Famous for outfitting classic American icons such as Bing Crosby, this 1950s golf brand has a full range of men's and women's clothing.

10 Bloomingdale's
MAP L2 ▪ 900 N. Michigan Ave.
An outpost of New York's homegrown department store that features in-store designer boutiques and a well-stocked shoe department.

Multi-level Bloomingdale's

Places to Eat and Drink

PRICE CATEGORIES
Price categories include a three-course meal for one, a glass of house wine, tax, and a 15–20 percent tip.

$ under $30 $$ $30–$60 $$$ over $60

Chefs at work, Nico Osteria

 Frontera Grill
MAP K3 ▪ 445 N. Clark St.
▪ 312-661-1434 ▪ Closed Sun & Mon
▪ Reservations only for groups of 5+
▪ $$
Chef Rick Bayless' regional Mexican cuisine warrants the two-margarita waits that inevitably face diners here.

2 NoMI
MAP L2 ▪ 800 N. Michigan Ave.
▪ 312-239-4030 ▪ $$$
On the seventh floor of the Park Hyatt Chicago, overlooking the landmark Water Tower, NoMI is a refined restaurant with a menu spanning sushi and steak.

 Signature Lounge
MAP L2
▪ 875 N. Michigan Ave.
▪ 312-787-9596 ▪ $$
Located on the 96th floor of the John Hancock Center, the Signature Lounge offers pricey cocktails and lofty views. No minors after 7pm.

GT Fish & Oyster

4 RL
MAP L2 ▪ 115 E. Chicago Ave.
▪ 312-475-1100 ▪ $$
This in-store steakhouse and power-eatery is furnished in upper-crust style by the Ralph Lauren Home shop while elegantly attired hostesses sport Polo.

5 Spiaggia
MAP L1 ▪ 980 N. Michigan Ave.
▪ 312-280-2750 ▪ $$
A special occasion restaurant, Spiaggia combines a romantic setting overlooking Oak Street Beach with sophisticated Italian food and a 700-vintage wine list.

6 Nico Osteria
MAP K1 ▪ 1015 N. Rush St.
▪ 312-994-7100 ▪ $$
This popular Italian seafood restaurant is run by famous chef Paul Kahan. The raw bar includes crudo and oysters.

7 Pump Room
MAP K1 ▪ 1301 N. State St.
▪ 312-229-6740 ▪ $$
A jazz trio, opulent decor, and a classic continental menu serve diners here. Celebrities love its famed "booth 1."

8 GT Fish & Oyster
MAP K3 ▪ 531 N. Wells St.
▪ 312-929-3501 ▪ $$
This seafood restaurant is one of the best in the city, providing elegant but unfussy food, including a raw bar and fixed-price offerings at lunch.

9 River Roast
MAP K3 ▪ 315 N. LaSalle St.
▪ 312-822-0100 ▪ $
Standing on the Chicago River, this bustling restaurant specializes in tasty roast chicken, served whole with crispy potatoes.

10 Zebra Lounge
MAP K2 ▪ 1220 N. State St.
▪ 312-642-5140
A classic piano lounge, the Zebra is intimate and decorated wall to wall in animal prints. It's a funky place to drink cocktails in the Gold Coast.

See map on p78

⌖10 Northside

Encompassing parts of Old Town, Lincoln Park, Lakeview, and Wrigleyville, Chicago's Northside boasts upscale restaurants and chi-chi boutiques galore, as well as some of the city's best bars and one of its most progressive theater companies, the Steppenwolf *(see p88)*. Older buildings have been transformed into beautiful condominiums, while stylish new apartments are springing up on empty lots. In season, nearby Wrigley Field fans bolster the lively Wrigleyville atmosphere by swarming the surrounding streets and bars. The vibrant gay hub of "Boystown" is also in this area, while running along Northside's eastern border is the incredible lakefront.

Rainbow pillar in Boystown

AREA MAP OF NORTHSIDE

1 Top 10 Sights
see pp87–9

1 Restaurants
see p93

1 Shops
see p90

1 Neighborhood Bars
see p92

1 Gay and Lesbian Bars
see p91

Chicago Cubs playing to a full house, Wrigley Field

1 Wrigley Field
MAP D1 ■ 1060 W. Addison St.
■ 1-773-404-2827 ■ Tours daily, $25
■ Adm ■ DA ■ www.cubs.com

Built in 1914, this is the USA's oldest National League baseball park. The home team, the Chicago Cubs, haven't won a World Series championship since 1908 (before the field even existed), but that doesn't stop Northsiders from being behind them every step of the way. In season (March–September), spending an afternoon cheering on the "Cubbies" in this marvelous stadium, with its ivy-clad walls, is a quintessential Chicago experience.

2 Chicago History Museum
MAP F4 ■ 1601 N. Clark St.
■ Open 9:30am–4:30pm Mon–Sat, noon–5pm Sun ■ Adm ■ DA

Focusing on Illinois and Chicago history since settler days, this museum was established in 1856 and is the city's oldest cultural institution. One of the society's first donors bequeathed his collection of Lincoln memorabilia: the ex-president's deathbed is one of the items displayed. Visitors can climb aboard the Pioneer locomotive, while events such as the World's Columbian Exposition and the Great Chicago Fire (see p40), are brought to life by photographs, decorative arts, and other exhibits. There is also a collection of costumes from the mid-18th century to the present, belonging to famous figures, from George Washington to Michael Jordan.

3 Boystown
MAP E1–2 ■ N. Halsted St.
(& much of Broadway) from Belmont Ave. to Grace St., & Clark St. from Belmont to Addison Aves

Strolling down North Halsted Street, it's fairly evident you're in Chicago's gay neighborhood when you hit shops called Gay Mart and Cupid's Treasure. Just 30 years ago, this area – officially East Lakeview – was pretty shabby, the bars were without signs, and parking was a cinch. But now buzzing Boystown is gay central – by day and by night.

Peggy Notebaert Nature Museum

4 Peggy Notebaert Nature Museum
MAP F3 ■ 2430 N. Cannon Dr. ■ 1-773-755-5100 ■ Open 9am–5pm Mon–Fri, 10am–5pm Sat & Sun ■ Adm ■ DA

This museum's sloping, beige exterior was inspired by the sand dunes that once occupied its site. Inside are a host of engrossing interactive exhibits, the highlight being the walk-through Butterfly Haven.

⑤ Armitage/Halsted Shopping District

MAP E4 ■ Armitage Ave. from Halsted St. to Racine Ave., & Halsted St. from Webster to Armitage Aves

This area of unique boutiques is a boon for fashionistas. Dozens of shops here sell everything from sophisticated evening wear to high-end accessories. Many of the stores occupy renovated Victorian town homes, which are set along pretty, tree-lined streets.

Lion enclosure, Lincoln Park Zoo

⑥ Lincoln Park Conservatory

MAP F3 ■ 2391 N. Stockton Dr. ■ Open 9am–5pm daily ■ DA

Take a free trip to the tropics at this spacious conservatory, just next to Lincoln Park Zoo. Opened in 1893, the glass structure is a year-round, 80° F (40° C) sanctuary from Chicago's bustle, and offers a welcome respite from the city's long winters. Paths meander past lush palms, flourishing ferns, and exquisite 100-year-old orchids. Avoid the crowds by coming on a weekday when, unless a seasonal show is taking place, it's a quiet space, with trickling water as the only background sound.

⑦ Lincoln Park Zoo

Who's watching who at this beloved city zoo, which attracts more than three million visitors annually (see pp30–31).

⑧ Steppenwolf Theatre Co.

MAP E4 ■ 1650 N. Halsted St. ■ 312-335-2650 ■ www.steppenwolf.org

Founded in 1974 in a church basement, this theater company grew quickly to include a corps of actors who would become famous on stage and screen, including John Malkovich and Gary Sinise. Now based in a modern complex with two full stages and a smaller Garage Theater, Steppenwolf has sent many hits to New York's Broadway over the years.

Lush gardens in front of Lincoln Park Conservatory

⑨ North Avenue Beach
MAP F4 ■ Lakeshore Dr. &
North Ave. ■ Open dawn to dusk
■ Lifeguards on duty from Memorial
Day–Labor Day

When summer graces Chicago with
its presence, locals of all ages and
nationalities converge on this short,
but inviting beach. Running along its
edge is the lakefront path, where
cyclists, in-line skaters, runners, and
walkers stream by. Confident folks
strut their stuff at the outdoor gym,
sand volleyball courts allow the
energetic to let off steam, and the
rooftop bar of the steamship-shaped
beach house is perfect for a drink
while watching the activity below.

Jogging, North Avenue Beach

⑩ Second City
MAP F4 ■ 1616 N. Wells St. ■
312-337-3992 ■ www.secondcity.com

It's hard to overstate the influence
that Second City has had on comedy
in America since it opened it doors
at North Wells Street in 1959. The
home of improvisational comedy,
Second City has been the starting
point for an army of talent from
John Belushi and Bill Murray to
Tina Fey, Dan Aykroyd, and Stephen
Colbert, and entire casts of the
popular TV show *Saturday Night Live*.
On two stages at its headquarters in
Old Town, Second City offers full-
length shows (another venue, UP
Comedy Club on West North Avenue,
is reserved for stand-up comedy).
Improv seating is first come first
served and tight, which just makes
the hilarity even more contagious.

EXPLORING NORTHSIDE

▶ **MORNING**

Fuel up for the day at one of
Lincoln Park's favorite breakfast
joints, **Frances'** (2552 N. Clark
St.), where they serve a
wonderfully fluffy French toast.
Afterwards, take a stroll east
down Wrightwood Avenue and
keep walking until you come to
the **Lincoln Park Zoo** *(see pp30–
31)*, where you can ride on the
wild side on the African Safari
motion simulator. Then meet all
the animals before breaking for
lunch with a view at **Café Brauer**,
built in 1908 by Prairie School
architect Dwight Perkins.

AFTERNOON

During warm weather, head to
the lakefront along Fullerton
Avenue where you can stroll, rent
bikes, sunbathe, or even brave
the chilly Lake Michigan waters.
In colder months, catch a bus
(nos. 22 or 151) and immerse
yourself in the **Chicago History
Museum** *(see p87)*, or take a five-
minute cab ride to **Armitage/
Halsted Shopping District** *(see
p88)* for classy retail therapy.

EVENING

This part of town has an
abundance of good eateries: hop
the "L" four stops or cab it to try
Mia Francesca's *(see p93)*, a lively
Italian trattoria where the pasta
dishes are big enough for two,
and there's an excellent wine list.
Round off your day with a visit to
Kingston Mines *(see p56)* – just a
short cab-ride away – to hear some
of the city's best blues musicians.

See map on p86e ←

Shops

1 **Architectural Artifacts**
MAP B3 ■ 4325 N.
Ravenswood Ave.

This huge warehouse stocks cast-offs from period homes, factories, and offices. Interesting pieces, from old wooden doors to models used to make rubber gloves, offer a down-the-rabbit-hole retail experience.

2 **Paper Source**
MAP D1 ■ 3543 N.
Southport Ave.

Originally an artist's supply store, Paper Source now concentrates on stationery and paper goods, from origami papers and individual handmade gift-wrap sheets to stylish notecards and greeting cards. A craft area offers workshops in card making.

3 **Lori's Designer Shoes**
MAP E4 ■ 824 W. Armitage Ave.

Devoted shoe hounds flock to this Lincoln Park store for its hot styles at discounted prices. The floors and walls are stacked high with boxes for handy self-serve try-on access.

4 **Art Effect**
MAP E4 ■ 934 W.
Armitage Ave.

An institution on trendy Armitage Avenue since 1984, this eclectic boutique offers a little bit of everything, from offbeat fashions, accessories and statement jewelry to retro kids' toys and unusual homewares.

A quirky item for sale at Art Effect

5 **Beatnix**
MAP E2 ■ 3400 N. Halsted St.

This store boasts the best supply of costumes and vintage gear in the city, including wigs, distinctive mod jewelry, and make-up.

6 **Andersonville Galleria**
MAP B3 ■ 5247 N. Clark St.

Artists, jewelers, fashion designers, knitters, and more maintain booths

Unabridged Bookstore

at Andersonville Galleria, a creative co-op. You could easily spend a few hours wandering around the three-story maze.

7 **Unabridged Bookstore**
MAP E2 ■ 3521 N. Broadway

Known for its large gay and lesbian section, this Boystown (see p87) bookstore also stocks books of all types, particularly kids' and Spanish-language books.

8 **Scout Chicago**
MAP B3 ■ 5221 N. Clark St.

An antique shop with a funky flare for mid-century modern and industrial one-offs, Scout always stocks surprises such as old gym lockers, in cramped but intriguing quarters.

9 **Uncle Dan's**
MAP D1 ■ 3551 N.
Southport Ave.

An outdoors equipment store with urban style that offers everything from mummy bags and tents to street-smart parkas that won't make you look like the Michelin man. There's a great selection of backpacks, too.

10 **Brimfield**
MAP B3 ■ 5219 N. Clark St.

Another of Andersonville's stylish vintage shops, Brimfield specializes in woolly plaids, from throw blankets to upholstered armchairs. Retro decorative items make browsing fun.

Gay and Lesbian Bars

① Second Story Bar
MAP L3 ■ 150 E. Ohio St.

This intimate bar that serves stiff drinks is a great evening escape. Its friendly atmosphere (and small size) encourages visitors to mix.

② The Closet
MAP E2 ■ 3325 N. Broadway

This dance club attracts a mostly lesbian crowd, but gay men and straight couples also groove to R&B, rap, dance, and diva videos.

③ Roscoe's Tavern
MAP E2 ■ 3356 N. Halsted St.

A young, preppy set packs this neighborhood bar for its antique decor, cozy fireplace, cheesy dance tunes, and, in summer, beer garden.

④ Sidetrack
MAP E2 ■ 3349 N. Halsted St.

Find some of the best cruising at this vast, four-room bar with more than two dozen video monitors that highlight a different theme (like show tunes or 1980s music) every night.

⑤ Kit Kat Lounge & Supper Club
MAP E2 ■ 3700 N. Halsted St. ■ Open dinner daily, Sun brunch

Martinis come in 52 flavors at this chic spot, where female impersonators show their lip-synching talent.

⑥ Big Chick's
MAP B3 ■ 5024 N. Sheridan Rd.

In a world of LGBT bars dominated by men, Big Chick's welcomes all persuasions. Themed events include trivia night and Bear Den night.

⑦ Berlin
MAP E2 ■ 954 W. Belmont Ave.

This edgy club attracts every type from straight girls to drag queens. After midnight, the dance floor hits its peak, rocking with a stellar sound system and light show.

⑧ Progress Bar
MAP E2 ■ 3359 N. Halsted St.

This sleek lounge is ideal for sipping must-try martinis while Boystown people-watching through wall-to-wall windows.

⑨ Crew Bar & Grill
MAP E2 ■ 4804 N. Broadway

With 20 enormous HDTVs, you'll always find a good spot to catch a game at this premier gay sports bar.

⑩ Hydrate
MAP E2 ■ 3458 N. Halsted St.

Hydrate features a bar in front with roll-up garage-style doors, and a dance floor out back that cranks into the early hours. A drag queen show "Beautie and Beaus" takes place on Saturday nights.

Pink lighting sets the mood, Kit Kat Lounge & Supper Club

See map on p86

Neighborhood Bars

Popular brewery Goose island

1 Goose Island
MAP D4 ▪ 1800 N. Clybourn Ave.

Though now owned by a brewing giant, Chicago's original microbrewery remains a local favorite, with a range of beer styles and a full menu to match. Brewery tours are offered on Saturday and Sunday.

2 Schubas Tavern and Harmony Grill
MAP D1 ▪ 3159 N. Southport Ave.

Twenty-somethings dress down for beer, live music, and a great restaurant that packs in crowds, especially on the patio during warm-weather weekends.

3 Murphy's Bleachers
MAP E1 ▪ 3655 N. Sheffield Ave.

Located just beyond the Wrigley Field, Murphy's Bleachers has a loyal following among Cubs fanatics as well as fair-weather drinkers.

4 Southport Lanes & Billiards
MAP D1 ▪ 3325 N. Southport Ave.

During the day, this is a laid-back bar: at night, a rowdy young crowd take turns at the four hand-set bowling lanes.

5 Village Tap
MAP D1 ▪ 2055 W. Roscoe St.

Popular for its seasonal back patio, the Village Tap in laid-back Roscoe Village offers a strong selection of tap beers and a good bar menu.

6 Gingerman Tavern
MAP D1 ▪ 3740 N. Clark St.

A Wrigleyville stalwart, Gingerman is not a sports bar despite being in the home of the Chicago Cubs . It has a range of beers and a few pool tables.

7 Delilah's
MAP D2 ▪ 2771 N. Lincoln Ave.

Declared one of "the great whiskey bars in the world" by *Whiskey Magazine*, Delilah's has been a neighborhood watering hole for years. It has some 400 different types of whiskeys on offer, not to mention many beers on tap.

8 Huettenbar
MAP B3 ▪ 4721 N. Lincoln Ave.

In the historically German district of Lincoln Square, Huettenbar channels old-world *gemeuthlichkeit*, or warmth, with flower-box-trimmed front windows, German beer on tap, and an Alpine mural behind the bar.

9 Half Acre Tap Room
MAP E3 ▪ 4257 N. Lincoln Ave.

The popular microbrewer Half Acre operates a neighborly taproom that usually features about 10 beers on tap for tasting. Guests can also get pitchers to go.

Cozy interior, Half Acre Tap Room

10 The Tin Lizzie
MAP E3 ▪ 2483 N. Clark St.

A sports bar-and-dance club, Tin Lizzie is packed wall-to-wall with twenty- to thirty-somethings most weekend nights, when DJs spin a variety of tunes.

Restaurants

PRICE CATEGORIES
Price categories include a three-course
meal for one, a glass of house wine, tax,
and a 15–20 percent tip.

$ under $30 $$ $30–$60 $$$ over $60

1 Alinea
MAP E4 ▪ 1723 N. Halsted St. ▪
312-867-0110 ▪ Closed lunch, Mon &
Tue ▪ DA (mention in advance) ▪ $$$
This high-end, fine-dining restaurant
serves delicious unique food pairings
in a very stylish setting.

2 Mia Francesca
MAP F4 ▪ 3311 N.
Clark St. ▪ 1-773-281-3310
▪ Open dinner daily,
10am–3pm Sat & Sun ▪ $$
The wait for the generous
portions of flavorful pastas,
seafood, and chicken at this
lively eatery is worth it.

3 Geja's Café
MAP E4 ▪ 340 W.
Armitage Ave. ▪ 1-773-281-
9101 ▪ Closed lunch
▪ No DA ▪ $$
The ultimate fondue in a
romantic setting. Choose cheese
or hot oil, or just opt for the divine
chocolate fondue.

4 Fish Bar
MAP E2 ▪ 2956 N. Sheffield
▪ 1-773-681-8177 ▪ Open 11:30am–
10pm Sun–Thu (to 12am Fri & Sat)
▪ $$
This small eatery serves the best
fish in the city – everything from
salmon, oysters, and tilapia to
classic fish and chips.

5 Yusho
MAP B4 ▪ 2853 N. Kedzie Ave.
▪ 1-773-904-8558 ▪ Closed lunch
(except Sun) ▪ $$
Highly regarded chef Mathias
Merges runs this casual Japanese
tavern with serious food ambitions.
Try the twice-fried chicken.

6 Longman & Eagle
MAP B4 ▪ 2657 N. Kedzie Ave.
▪ 1-773-276-7110 ▪ Open from 9am
daily ▪ $$
This funky place takes its farm-fresh
fare seriously but has a casual
atmosphere in two packed rooms.
No reservations; arrive early or wait.

7 North Pond
MAP F3 ▪ 2610 N. Cannon Dr.
▪ 1-773-477-5845 ▪ Open Wed–Sun
from 5:30pm, and Sun brunch ▪ $$
This pond-side restaurant (a former
skaters' "warming house") serves up
American gourmet cuisine.

North Pond's beautiful dining room

8 Lula Café
MAP B4 ▪ 2537 N. Kedzie Ave.
▪ 1-773-489-9554 ▪ Open 9am–2am
Wed–Mon ▪ $
An eclectic café in Logan Square,
Lula champions local and organic
ingredients in its farm-to-table meals,
from breakfast through to late night.

9 Ann Sather
MAP E2 ▪ 909 W. Belmont Ave.
▪ 1-773-348-2378 ▪ $
Known for its scrumptious
breakfasts, this Swedish restaurant
also serves lunchtime specialties.

10 Boka
MAP E4 ▪ 1729 N. Halsted St.
▪ 312-337-6070 ▪ Open from 5pm
daily ▪ $$
Boka offers elegant, seasonally
informed food in a series of rooms.

See map on p86

🔟 South Loop

Just south of the business-centric Loop, this sprawling area mixes ethnic enclaves such as Chinatown (founded in the 1870s by migrant transcontinental railroad workers) with upper crust addresses, built after the Great Chicago Fire of 1871 *(see p40)*.

The region has many Chicago "must-sees," but the jewel in the crown is undisputedly the impressive Museum Campus: here, the Field Museum, John G. Shedd Aquarium, and Adler Planetarium celebrate the wonders of the earth, sea, and sky respectively, collectively drawing over four million visitors each year. The highway that once separated the Field from its neighbors has been replaced by an inviting green campus, where cyclists and skaters join museum-goers on the plant-bordered paths in fair weather.

Figurine, Field Museum

Skeleton exhibits, Field Museum

1 Field Museum

One of the three lakefront institutions to occupy the Museum Campus, the vast Field Museum boasts a collection of more than 20 million fascinating natural history and anthropological artifacts from around the world *(see pp18–19)*.

2 Prairie Avenue District

MAP C5 ■ For walking tours (Jul–Sep) call 312-326-1480 ■ Clarke House: 1827 S. Indiana Ave.; tours noon & 2pm Wed–Sun; adm; DA ■ Glessner House: 1800 S. Prairie Ave.; tours 1 & 3pm Wed–Sun; adm; no DA

Of the wealthy enclaves both north and south of the Chicago River that

AREA MAP OF SOUTH LOOP

- **1** Top 10 Sights
  see pp94–7
- ① Places to Eat
  see p99
- ① Bars and Clubs
  see p98

grew up following the Great Fire of 1871, Prairie Avenue was the most fashionable and ritziest. Only a few mansions remain today, of which two are open to the public (tour only): the Romanesque-Revival 1887 Glessner House, and Chicago's oldest building – Clarke House – built in 1836.

③ Blues Heaven Foundation

MAP C5 ■ 2120 S. Michigan Ave.
■ For tours call 312-808-1286
■ Closed Sun ■ Adm ■ Limited DA

Located in the former studios of Chess Records, where blues greats from Muddy Waters to Willie Dixon once recorded, Blues Heaven has records, photos, and stage costumes dedicated to Chicago's blues style and its performers. The former label's music plays on the PA. There are occasional live performances.

Wild Reef exhibit, John G. Shedd Aquarium

④ John G. Shedd Aquarium

The second of the three Museum Campus sights, the Shedd is also one of the oldest and most visited public aquariums in the world. Dive in to discover the many treasures of the aquatic world on show (see pp28–9).

Star gazing, Adler Planetarium

5 Adler Planetarium

MAP M6 ■ 1300 S. Lake Shore Dr. ■ Open 9:30am–4pm Mon–Fri, 9:30am–4:30pm Sat & Sun; third Thu of month 6–10pm for "Adler After Dark" (over-21s only); for showtimes call 312-922-7827 ■ Adm ■ DA

The first planetarium in the Western Hemisphere completes the Museum Campus trio. Visit its numerous galleries to walk among the stars, explore the worlds that orbit the Sun, and be enlightened by 1,000 years of astronomical discovery. Don't miss the Sky Theater show, which is projected on the 68-ft (21-m) dome of the historic Zeiss planetarium. The virtual reality events in the StarRider Theater launch you into the outer reaches of space and even give you the chance to interact with the show via a panel in the armrest.

6 Museum of Contemporary Photography

MAP L5 ■ 600 S. Michigan Ave. ■ Open 10am–5pm, Mon–Sat (to 8pm Thu), noon–5pm Sun ■ DA ■ www.mocp.org

Run by and located in Columbia College Chicago, this museum is one of a kind in the Midwest. It exhibits the portfolios of international modern masters, with shows tending toward the experimental rather than the traditional documentary. Changing exhibitions also present a mixture of local talents and well-established ones, such as Gary Winogrand and William Eggleston. Frequent gallery talks give curators and artists the chance to discuss the shows with museum-goers.

7 Maxwell Street Market

MAP J6 ■ 548 W. Roosevelt Rd. ■ Open 7am–3pm Sun

Both 19th-century European immigrants and 20th-century African-American settlers fleeing the Deep South got their entrepreneurial start selling from pushcarts around Maxwell Street. In 1994 the market was relocated to make way for the new University of Illinois at Chicago and, while a shadow of its former self, it still makes for a vibrant Sunday morning. Do expect plenty of Mexican housewares and used tools. The occasional treasure, such as a vintage fur coat, does show up, however. Another reason to visit is to try the homemade tacos from the Mexican food stalls that line the street.

8 Northerly Island

MAP M6 ■ 1521 S. Linn White Dr. ■ 312-745-2910 ■ Open 6am–11pm ■ www.chicagoparkdistrict.com

Northerly Island was part of city planner Daniel Burnham's plan for the lakefront to include a series of offshore islands acting as parks. At Northerly Island, Burnham's vision is now a reality. The green space extending south of the Adler Planetarium is the city's newest lakefront park, which hosts native gardens carved with walking trails, and an outdoor concert stage.

Lakefront strolling, Northerly Island

9 Jane Addams Hull House
MAP H5 ▪ 800 S. Halsted St.
▪ 312-413-5353 ▪ Open 10am–4pm
Tue–Fri, noon–4pm Sun ▪ DA
▪ www.hullhousemuseum.org

When European immigrants were flooding Chicago to work in its rail and stock yards during the late 19th and early 20th centuries, Jane Addams bought Hull House for a specific purpose. From there, she offered social services and facilities to this immigrant working class, including day care, employment counselling, and art classes. Winner of the 1931 Nobel Peace Prize, Addams also championed the rights of women and helped usher in child labor laws. Her office, furnishings, and artwork are on display, and temporary exhibits tell the story of the settlement at Hull House and the invaluable work of its residents.

The famous Chinatown Gate

10 Chinatown
MAP B5 ▪ Around Wentworth
Ave. & Cermak Rd.

Crowned by the landmark Chinatown Gate spanning Wentworth Avenue, Chicago's Chinatown isn't that large – running roughly eight blocks – but it is colorful. Home to Chicago's oldest Asian community, Chinatown was founded in the 19th century by transcontinental railroad workers fleeing West Coast prejudice. Cantonese and Mandarin are still spoken far more widely here than English. Stroll Wentworth to see the ornate On Leong Tong Building, buy fresh almond cookies from Chinese bakeries, peruse the many import and herbal shops, or dine in one of the numerous local restaurants.

EXPLORING SOUTH LOOP

▶ **MORNING**

Start by grabbing coffee and an oreo cookie flapjack at **The Bongo Room** (1152 S. Wabash Ave., 312-291-0100). From there, walk through Grant Park to Museum Campus. Here you can choose between the **Field Museum** (see pp18–19), **Adler Planetarium**, and **John G. Shedd Aquarium** (see pp28–9). If you plan to visit other museums on your trip, it makes sense to purchase a CityPass (see p65). If you opt to see the highlights of each, end up at the Shedd, where the **Soundings** restaurant offers good food and great views overlooking the lake.

AFTERNOON

Hail a cab (plenty wait outside the museums) or walk to the nearby pedestrian bridge at 18th Street to get to the **Prairie Avenue District** (see pp94–5), where you can stroll the historic streets and maybe even catch the 3pm tour of the **Glessner House** (see p95). Muster energy to catch a cab to the **Adler Planetarium** and walk south, enjoying the skyline views from **Northerly Island**.

EVENING

Head over to Wabash Avenue for an early supper at one of the trendy eateries on what is now a burgeoning strip. A popular spot is **Gioco** (see p99), known for its stellar Italian fare (reservations are recommended). After dinner, go on to **Buddy Guy's Legends** (see p98) and hear the blues.

See map on pp94–5 ←

Bars and Clubs

(1) Reggie's
MAP K6 ▪ 2105 S. State St.
This rock venue and grill-pub offers nightly musical entertainment and good bar fare. Next door, Record Breakers sells rare vinyl and CDs.

(2) M Lounge
MAP K6 ▪ 1520 S. Wabash Ave.
Listen to traditional and modern jazz in style on comfy couches and low-slung seating in cranberry, chocolate, and sage. Stop by for live jazz on Wednesdays.

(3) Vintage Lounge
MAP G6 ▪ 1449 W. Taylor St.
The mahogany bar, classic cocktails, and chandeliers at Vintage Lounge will take you back to Old Chicago. A range of pizzas and homemade donuts are on the menu.

(4) Punch House
MAP B5 ▪ 1227 W. 18th St.
Hidden away in the basement of Dusek's restaurant, Punch House looks like a swinging 1970s recreation room. Potent punches are the specialty of the house.

(5) Buddy Guy's Legends
MAP L5 ▪ 700 S. Wabash Ave.
Run by bluesman Buddy Guy, this club is arguably the city's best. To get a table, come early and dine on decent barbecue food.

Buddy Guy's Legends

(6) Jazz Showcase
MAP K5 ▪ 806 S. Plymouth Ct.
Since 1947, this has been Chicago's premiere jazz showroom, hosting the greats past and present. Talkers will be shushed. Sunday afternoon shows are family friendly.

(7) Hackney's
MAP K5 ▪ 733 S. Dearborn St.
On Printer's Row, Hackney's offers classic pub grub, including burgers, as well as a good selection of tap beer and a popular patio in season.

(8) Cetta's
MAP G6 ▪ 1358 W. Taylor St.
▪ Closed Sun
This dark, intimate Little Italy hideaway is a great place to cozy as a couple before or after dinner with one of forty by-the-glass wines. There is live music on Friday nights.

(9) Tufano's Vernon Park Tap
MAP H5 ▪ 1073 W. Vernon Park Pl. ▪ Closed Mon
Also known as Tufano's, this popular bar has legions of local and celebrity fans who pile in for house wine and generous, inexpensive pastas.

(10) Hawkeye's Bar & Grill
MAP G6 ▪ 1458 W. Taylor St.
Try this sports bar for beer-fueled camaraderie and a genuine slice of Chicago fan zeal. A shuttle bus even delivers patrons to the United Center and US Cellular Field.

Places to Eat

PRICE CATEGORIES
Price categories include a three-course meal for one, a glass of house wine, tax, and a 15–20 percent tip.

$ under $30 $$ $30–$60 $$$ over $60

The informal Eleven City Diner

① Eleven City Diner
MAP L6 ■ 1112 S. Wabash Ave.
■ 312-212-1112 ■ $

Deli meets diner here, and breakfast is served all day. Come for sizeable sandwiches and old-fashioned fountain drinks such as egg cream.

② Gioco
MAP K6 ■ 1312 S. Wabash Ave.
■ 312-939-3870 ■ Closed lunch Sat & Sun ■ $$

Rustic Italian food is the draw at Gioco, a one-time speakeasy.

③ Pompei Bakery
MAP G6 ■ 1531 W. Taylor St.
■ 312-421-5179 ■ No reservations ■ $

This Little Italy lunch spot showcases a dozen delicious by-the-slice pizzas. Hot sandwiches and stuffed pastas round out the offerings.

④ Acadia
MAP L6 ■ 1639 S. Wabash Ave.
■ 312-360-9500 ■ Closed lunch ■ $$$

Acadia takes its cue from Maine, offering a fine lobster roll. Tasting menus come in five and ten courses.

⑤ Davanti Enoteca
MAP G6 ■ 1359 W. Taylor St. ■ 312-226-5550 ■ Closed Mon–Thu ■ $$

A charming wine bar and restaurant in Little Italy, Davanti Enoteca serves small plate starters, sharable larger plates including pastas and pizzas, and entrées such as grilled swordfish.

⑥ Chez Joel
MAP H6 ■ 1119 W. Taylor St.
■ 312-226-6479 ■ Closed Mon & lunch Sun ■ $$

A quaint French bistro in the heart of Little Italy charms fans with its sunny decor and fine classics.

⑦ Francesca's on Taylor
MAP G6 ■ 1400 W. Taylor St. ■ 312-829-2828 ■ Closed lunch Sun ■ $

The Little Italy branch of Wrigleyville's Mia Francesca offers generous portions of refined Italian cuisine at reasonable prices.

⑧ Phoenix
MAP A6 ■ 2131 S. Archer Ave.
■ 312-328-0848 ■ $

Phoenix attracts dim sum diners from near and far. Go early on weekends or prepare for long waits.

Diners enjoying dim sum at Phoenix

⑨ Rosebud Cafe
MAP G6 ■ 1500 W. Taylor St.
■ 312-942-1117 ■ $$

The Italian cooking at Rosebud's, located in Little Italy, isn't daring but its convivial vibe is hard to resist. Long waits for tables are common.

⑩ Mercat a la Planxa
MAP L5 ■ 638 S. Michigan Ave.
■ 312-765-0524 ■ $$

Arguably the city's best Spanish restaurant, lively Mercat a la Planxa specializes in tapas such as bacon-wrapped dates and juicy lamb chops. Order suckling pig 72 hours ahead.

See map on pp94–5

TOP10 Far South

With magnificent architecture, interesting ethnic enclaves, and stand-out museums, Chicago's Far South encompasses districts such as Hyde Park and Kenwood that merit a journey off the beaten tourist path – despite being bordered to the south by some less-than-welcoming neighborhoods.

Hyde Park and Kenwood began life as suburbs for the wealthy escaping the dirty city; today, this part of town is a fascinating melting pot of University of Chicago students and Mexican, Asian, African-American, and Indian residents. Recreation and leisure opportunities abound on spectacular tracts of green space, including the University of Chicago's Midway Plaisance and Jackson Park, site of the 1893 World's Columbian Exposition *(see p23)*.

Detail of a relief, Oriental Institute

AREA MAP OF FAR SOUTH

Far South

1 **Top 10 Sights**
see pp101–103

① **Places to Eat**
see p105

① **Shops**
see p104

University of Chicago campus

① University of Chicago

MAP E6 ▪ 5801 S. Ellis Ave.
▪ Metra station: 55th St. ▪ 1-773-
702-1234 ▪ www.uchicago.edu

Noted for its research and high
educational standards, this
remarkable private university has
produced over 80 Nobel Prize
winning alumni and staff (see p50).

② DuSable Museum of African American History

MAP D5 ▪ 740 E. 56th Pl. ▪ Open
10am–5pm Tue–Sat, noon–5pm Sun
▪ Adm (free Sun) ▪ DA
▪ www.dusablemuseum.org

Located on the eastern edge of
Washington Park, this museum is
named after Chicago's first non-
native settler, Jean Baptiste Point
du Sable. The permanent exhibits
celebrate other firsts, such as the
first black US astronaut, Major
Robert Lawrence, and Chicago's first
African-American mayor, Harold
Washington. Thought-provoking
exhibits include rusted slave shackles
and the "Freedom Now" mural,
depicting 400 years of African-
American history from the early days
of slavery to Civil Rights marches.

③ Stony Island Arts Bank

MAP F6 ▪ 6760 S. Stony Island
Ave. ▪ 312-857-5561 ▪ Open 11am–
6pm Tue–Sat ▪ DA

In 2015, contemporary artist Theaster
Gates, Jr. converted this once-grand
1893 bank into an exhibition and arts
space, fostering gentrification in a
region much in need of investment.
The center houses the record
collection of the late Chicago DJ
Frankie Knuckles, considered the
father of House music, and over
60,000 glass lantern slides from the
art history department at the
University of Chicago. Both collections
can be visited during free hour-long
tours offered every Saturday at 1pm.

Exhibits at the DuSable Museum

4 Oriental Institute
MAP E6 ■ 1155 E. 58th St.
■ 10am–5pm Tue & Thu–Sun (to 8pm Wed) ■ DA ■ www.oi.uchicago.edu

Learn about the origins of agriculture, the invention of writing, the birth of civilization, and the beginning of the study of arts, science, politics, and religion at this University of Chicago museum. Five galleries showcase ancient Near Eastern civilizations from about 3500 BC to AD 100; most exhibits were unearthed during the department's own excavations.

Museum of Science and Industry

5 Museum of Science and Industry
The largest science museum within a single building in the Western Hemisphere, this popular museum attracts over two million people a year *(see pp20–21)*.

6 Kenwood Historic District
MAP E5 ■ Boundaries: E. 43rd St. (north), E. 51st St. (south), S. Blackstone Ave. (east), and S. Drexel Blvd. (west)

This wealthy enclave within Kenwood, founded by John A. Kennicott in 1856, has mansions that must be seen to be believed. In the late 19th century this area was an upscale Chicago suburb, where wealthy residents built majestic homes on spacious lots, a rarity in the quickly booming city. A stroll around the district uncovers architectural styles ranging from Italianate and Colonial Revival to Prairie style, by influential figures such as Howard Van Doren Shaw and Frank Lloyd Wright *(see pp36–7)*.

7 Robie House
MAP E6 ■ 5757 S. Woodlawn Ave. ■ Tour times and prices vary; for information and to buy tickets, call 312-994-4000 or visit www.gowright. org ■ No DA

This splendid 1910 residence by Frank Lloyd Wright is easily spotted by its steel-beam roof, which overhangs the building by 20 ft (6 m) at each end. Take a tour through its low-ceilinged interior, past more than 170 art-glass windows and doors, to gain insight into the ten-year restoration program. The building was a private home until 1926, when it became a dormitory for the Chicago Theological Seminary. It was later bought by a development firm, who donated it to the University of Chicago in 1963, the same year it was designated a National Historic Landmark.

8 Osaka Japanese Gardens
MAP F6 ■ Jackson Park, 58th St. & Lake Shore Dr. ■ Open dawn–dusk ■ DA

At the north end of Jackson Park's serene Wooded Island (excellent for bird-watching) lies this hushed retreat, complete with meandering paths, lagoons, and fountains. The garden is a partial re-creation of the one formed in 1934 around the beautiful Japanese Pavilion built for the 1893 Expo, which sadly burned down in 1946. The gardens were renamed in 1993 for one of Chicago's sister cities, Osaka, which donated the Japanese gate seen here.

Decorative bridges cross the lagoon, Osa

Getting To and
  Around Chicago   **108**

Practical Information   **110**

Places to Stay   **116**

General Index   **120**

Acknowledgments   **126**

Getting To and Around Chicago

Arriving by Air

Most international and many domestic flights arrive at **O'Hare International Airport**, one of the world's busiest airports, located 20 miles (32 km) northwest of downtown Chicago. Serving most major airlines, including most international flights, this big and sprawling airport offers free transportation between its four terminals via the Airport Transport System (ATS) train.

The Chicago Transit Authority's Blue Line "L" train connects O'Hare to downtown; follow airport signs that say "Trains to City." Trips take about 30 minutes. Taxis are available from the lower arrivals level of each terminal. When the roads are clear it can take 40 minutes to reach downtown, but time can quickly double with traffic.

Car rental agencies are located near the baggage claim areas in terminals 1–3, and via courtesy telephones from terminal 5 (do not be confused by the numbering; there is no terminal 4 at O'Hare).

Midway International Airport is Chicago's second airport. Located 10 miles (16 km) south-west of downtown, it serves mostly domestic airlines, including several popular budget carriers such as Southwest Airlines. Taxis are available from the lower arrivals level; car rental agencies are located in the main terminal building; and shuttle

buses leave from in front of it. The CTA's Orange Line "L" connects Midway and downtown in trips of less than 30 minutes.

Available near baggage reclaim at both airports, **GO Airport Express** will drop off (and pick up) at any requested downtown location; book the return airport shuttle in advance. Several companies, including **Elite Chicago Limo**, offer private door-to-door services booked in advance at rates that are higher than taxis.

Arriving by Train

Up to 56 **Amtrak** trains serve Union Station in downtown each day, ranging from cross-country routes to a commuter service to nearby Milwaukee. The nearest "L" stop to Union station is at Clinton, but it's a good walk, so it is often better to take a cab or bus to your destination.

Arriving by Road

The inexpensive **Megabus** links Chicago with lots of other Midwestern cities, and the bus stop is directly opposite Union Station. Tickets must be booked online and are not sold by the driver or on the bus. **Greyhound** buses offer service throughout the country from its terminal in the South Loop, where travelers can walk up and buy tickets.

Those arriving by car generally do so via the busy Interstate highways, including I-55 from the

southwest, I-57 from the south, I-88 from the west, I-90 from the east and northwest, and I-94 from the east and north. Route 66 from Santa Monica, CA joins I-55 before hitting downtown Chicago.

Getting Around by Train

Short for elevated train, the "L" is nevertheless the name given to the entire **Chicago Transit Authority** (CTA) train network, including the sections that travel underground. The eight lines are identifiable by color: red, green, blue, brown, orange, pink, purple, and yellow. The red and blue lines run 24 hours a day (less often off-peak). Trains arrive every 5 to 20 minutes, and the service is fast and economical. Its smartphone app provides real-time schedules.

Metra, the commuter rail system, serves the city's suburbs. Downtown stops are Union Station, LaSalle Street Station, Ogilvie Transportation Center, and Randolph Street Station.

By Bus

The CTA bus network covers the entire city and the suburbs, and is especially useful for reaching the lakefront, which is not served by the "L". Keep an eye out for the blue and white bus stop signs.

PACE buses also service the city suburbs and are numbered 208 and higher.

Tickets

The regular "L" or bus fare is $2.25, with an extra 25¢ for a transfer card (valid for two transfers within two hours of purchase), and you need exact change. You can buy a Ventra transit card with a preset value or a top-up Transit card and charge it with the desired amount at an automated vending machine at any station. The relevant fare is then deducted from your pass each time you take a ride. You can buy 1- to 7-day CTA Passes from over 1,000 retail locations including drug stores and Currency Exchanges.

Metra fares vary according to the journey's length. Tickets may be purchased at automated kiosks at each station.

By Taxi

It is usually easy to hail a cab downtown and in popular neighborhoods in commercial areas; in residential districts, it's better to call for one. There's an initial charge, then a fee per mile and per extra passenger. A 10–15 percent tip is expected. Companies include: **Checker Taxi Assoc., Flash Cab Co.,** and **Yellow Cab Co.** The ride-sharing service **Uber** is also popular, summoning a driver using their personal car. Users can only access Uber drivers using the smartphone app.

May through September, **Chicago Water Taxi** runs boats between the Wrigley Building and a stop for both Union Station and the Ogilvie Transportation Center. **Shoreline Water Taxis** also offer a frequent service on the Chicago River to Willis Tower as well as on Lake Michigan from Navy Pier to the John G. Shedd Aquarium.

By Car

Driving in the city is not recommended. Parking is difficult to find and often expensive, and heavy traffic is common. Those arriving by car are advised to leave their vehicle in a parking lot and use public transportation or taxis to get around. However, for those who would like to get beyond the metropolitan area, the car-share service **Zipcar** offers rentals by the hour or by the day. Members should apply online prior to reserving a car; charges include gas and insurance.

By Bicycle

Chicago has more than 200 miles (322 km) of bike lanes in its city streets, and encourages short commutes via cycle with its bike-share service, **Divvy**. Riders can purchase a 24-hour pass for $9.95 at any of the hundreds of Divvy bike stations around the 18 miles (29 km) of lakefront bike paths.

On Foot

The best way to explore Chicago, particularly downtown and Northside areas (including the Mag Mile and Lincoln Park), is by walking. Avoid south of the South Loop after dark.

DIRECTORY

ARRIVING BY AIR
Elite Chicago Limo
W elitechicagolimo.com

GO Airport Express
W airportexpress.com

Midway International Airport
W flychicago.com/midway

O'Hare International Airport
W flychicago.com/ohare

ARRIVING BY TRAIN
Amtrak
W amtrak.com

ARRIVING BY ROAD
Greyhound
W greyhound.com

Megabus
W us.megabus.com

TRAIN AND BUS
Chicago Transit Authority
W transitchicago.com

Metra
W metrarail.com

PACE
W pacebus.com

TAXI
Checker Taxi Assoc.
W checkertaxichicago.com

Chicago Water Taxi
W chicagowatertaxi.com

Flash Cab Co.
W flashcab.com

Shoreline Water Taxis
W shorelinesightseeing.com

Uber
W uber.com

Yellow Cab Co.
W yellowcabchicago.com

CAR
Zipcar
W zipcar.com

BICYCLE
Divvy
W divvybikes.com

Practical Information

Passports and Visas

Citizens of EU countries, Australia, Chile, Iceland, New Zealand, and Japan can spend up to 90 days in the US without a visa, so long as they have a valid passport and a round-trip ticket. They will also need to register with the **US Department of Homeland Security** and pay a fee online prior to departure. Canadian citizens must show a valid passport. Citizens of other countries should contact their local US embassy well in advance of their trip to obtain the relevant visa.

Customs and Immigration

Landing cards and customs forms are distributed on the plane. Often travelers will also be required to enter such information on a computer screen in the entry hall. Foreign nationals have to join a separate line to have these and their passports inspected after landing. Strict security checks, involving the taking of photographs and fingerprints, are now in place for those arriving in the US on a visa. Note that any person entering the US is required to stay off their cell phones while in the immigration line.

US Customs and Border Protection stipulates that visitors can bring up to $100 of merchandize as gifts per family duty-free. The $100 cap may include 100 cigars but no alcohol.

Travel Safety Advice

Visitors can get up-to-date travel safety information from the **Foreign and Commonwealth Office** in the UK, the **State Department** in the US, and the **Department of Foreign Affairs and Trade** in Australia.

Travel Insurance

A comprehensive travel insurance policy is recommended. This should include cover for trip cancellation, lost luggage, car rental insurance and medical expenses, which are high in America.

Rental car agencies offer vehicle coverage (which can be high), but many credit cards, home owner's insurance policies, and banks extend vehicle coverage. Check with your credit card, insurer or bank before leaving home.

Emergency Services

For police, fire, and medical emergencies, dial 911. If you are not in a position to speak, the emergency locator should still be able to track you. For non-emergency police matters, such as theft or vandalism, dial 311 to reach the City Helpline. Both numbers can be accessed by cell phones.

Health

Tap water is potable and special vaccinations are not required. Carry with you prescriptions for medications that you take.

For serious illnesses, see the hospitals and emergency rooms listed in the Yellow Pages of the telephone directory. **Weiss Memorial Hospital** and **Northwestern Memorial Hospital** are convenient to downtown and the city's Northside, while **Bernard A. Mitchell Hospital**, at the University of Chicago, serves the South Side.

Even with medical insurance, you may have to pay for services and claim reimbursement after. Contact your insurer before receiving any treatment. Many dental clinics are open 24 hours and available for emergency procedures. Check with the hotel concierge or contact the **Chicago Dental Society** for a referral.

Pharmacies are plentiful throughout the city. Many drug stores are open 24 hours. The most popular drug store chains, including **Walgreens** and **CVS**, all have pharmacies inside. The pharmacies, however, even in 24-hour drug stores, are often only open during regular business hours and often close on Sunday.

Chicago is a city of extreme seasons. Visitors should be prepared for cold, windy, and snowy winters, which can create hazardous conditions. A hat, gloves, and suitable footwear are essential. In summer, the extreme heat can also cause health problems: ensure you apply sunscreen, wear a hat, and drink plenty of water.

Personal Security

As in most cities, the most common crimes are pickpocketing and purse snatching. Common sense can help deter these problems. Leave surplus cash, credit cards, and valuables in a safe place at your hotel, preferably a locked safe in the room. Don't walk around with your wallet in a back pocket, and keep bags securely fastened and close to your body. Keep a copy of your credit card numbers (and the number to call if they are lost) separate from the cards, and bring with you photocopies of important documents, including passports, in case they are stolen.

It's best to avoid using public transportation very late at night. Take a taxi instead. Train platforms and trains usually have an intercom in case of emergency. At night, avoid walking alone in dimly lit areas and in parks. Steer clear of areas on the far West Side of the city and parts of the South Side where crime levels are much higher.

Currency and Banking

The US currency is the dollar ($), which is divided into 100 cents. Paper notes are in denominations of $1, $5, $10, $20, $50, and $100. Coins are 50 cents, 25 cents, 10 cents, 5 cents, and 1 penny. Coins valued at $1 and $2 are in circulation, but are very rarely used.

ATMs (cash machines) abound and are the easiest way to get money, though most banks charge a fee for use and another for the exchange rate. The machines will list the fees and ask you if you wish to accept them before continuing with the transaction.

Banks tend to offer better exchange rates than the exchange windows found at the airports, though rates vary from bank to bank and not all banks offer foreign exchanges.

As an emergency stash, US dollar traveler's checks can be changed at most banks and foreign exchanges by showing a photo ID. They can also normally be used in stores and restaurants.

Credit cards are widely accepted and commonly used, even for small purchases like a coffee. Some smaller, family-run establishments only accept cash, but those with this policy usually advertise this clearly, often with signs in their windows.

DIRECTORY

PASSPORTS AND VISAS

US Department of Homeland Security
🌐 esta.cbp.dhs.gov

EMBASSIES AND CONSULATES

Australia
MAP J4 ■ 123 N. Wacker Dr. 📞 312-419-1480
🌐 usa.embassy.gov.au

Canada
MAP L4 ■ 180 N. Stetson Ave.
📞 312-616-1860
🌐 chicago.gc.ca

Ireland
MAP K3 ■ 1 E. Wacker Dr.
📞 312-337-2700
🌐 irishconsulate.org

New Zealand
🌐 nzembassy.com

UK
MAP L3 ■ 625 N. Michigan Ave.
📞 312-970-3800
🌐 gov.uk

CUSTOMS AND IMMIGRATION

US Customs and Border Protection
🌐 cbp.gov

TRAVEL SAFETY ADVICE

Department of Foreign Affairs and Trade
🌐 dfat-gov-au
🌐 smartraveller.gov.au

Foreign and Commonwealth Office
🌐 gov.uk/foreign-travel-advice

US State Department
🌐 travel.state.gov

HEALTH

Bernard A. Mitchell Hospital
MAP E6 ■ 5841 S. Maryland Ave.
📞 1-773-702-1000
🌐 uchospitals.edu

Chicago Dental Society
📞 312-836-7300
🌐 cds.org

CVS
🌐 cvs.com

Northwestern Memorial Hospital
MAP L2 ■ 201 E. Huron St.
📞 312-926-3627
🌐 nm.org

Walgreens
🌐 walgreens.com

Weiss Memorial Hospital
4646 N. Marine Dr.
📞 1-773-878-8700
🌐 weisshospital.com

Internet and Telephone

Many cafes and hotels offer free Wi-Fi, usually accessible by a password available for the asking. The City of Chicago offers free public Wi-Fi in hotspots around the city, including all 79 Chicago Public Library locations, the Cultural Center (see p71), Daley Plaza (see p75), and Millennium Park (see pp34–5).

Chicago has two area codes: 312 for downtown and the immediate vicinity; 773 for the rest of the city, including the Northside and South Side. Dial 1 + the area code for any US number outside the area code you are in; cell phones do not require a 1 before the full number, including the area code. To dial abroad, key in 011 + country code + city code (omitting any initial 0).

Public phones, which accept both coins and credit cards, are fast disappearing in the wake of cell phone ubiquity. Most mobile phones work in America if unlocked by your carrier. Check the costs and data packages available before you travel, or consider buying a local SIM card to avoid high roaming charges.

Postal Services

Most branches of the **US Postal Service** are open 9am–6pm Monday to Friday and 9am–1pm Saturday. Some neighbourhood locations may have more abbreviated hours, and others may also be open for a few hours on Sunday morning. Many stores, including grocery stores and drug stores, sell stamps. Mailboxes are navy blue and posted on many street corners.

Television and Radio

For local TV, there's a wide range to choose from: CBS (Channel 2); NBC (Channel 5); ABC (Channel 7); WGN (Channel 9); WTTW Public TV (Channel 11); and Fox (Channel 32). Most TVs also offer a wide range of cable TV programming.

The most popular radio stations include: WFMT (98.7 FM) for classical, WLUP (97.9 FM) for rock, WGCI (107.5 FM) for R&B, and WXRT (93.1 FM) for adult alternative. WBBM (780 AM) is a news station, as is Chicago Public Radio WBEZ (91.5 FM), and WSCR (670 AM) covers sports.

Newspapers and Magazines

The city's two main daily newspapers are the Chicago Tribune and the Chicago Sun-Times. Both are widely available, and also offer their news stories online. The free alternative weekly The Reader offers local arts, dining and theater reviews plus lifestyle and political stories, as does the monthly magazine Chicago Magazine. The online-only magazine Time Out Chicago offers good suggestions for entertainment and dining.

Opening Hours

Office hours for businesses are generally 9am–5pm Monday to Friday. Shop and mall hours can vary but they are usually open 10am–9pm Monday to Saturday and noon–5pm Sunday. However, Northside boutiques and stores along the Mag Mile often stay open until 7 or 8pm nightly, except on Sunday.

Banks are usually open during regular office hours only, which is normally 9am–5pm Monday to Friday, though most banks offer 24-hour access to ATM machines, many times in indoor halls that require you to swipe your bank card to gain admission.

Museums and attractions keep their own various hours, though many extend their hours during the summer season and some offer at least one evening with extended opening hours each week. It is best to consult their websites before going to avoid disappointment.

Most banks, shops, offices, and attractions are closed over public holidays including New Year's Day (Jan 1); Martin Luther King Day (3rd Mon in Jan); President's Day (3rd Mon in Feb); Casimir Pulaski Day (1st Mon in Mar); Memorial Day (last Mon in May); Independence Day (July 4); Labor Day (1st Mon in Sep); Thanksgiving (4th Thu in Nov); and Christmas Day (Dec 25).

Time Difference

Chicago operates on Central Time (6 hours behind GMT). Daylight savings time begins at 3am on the first Sunday in April, when the clocks are moved forward an hour, and reverts to standard time at 1am on the last Sunday in October when they are then moved back an hour.

Electrical Appliances

Electrical appliances in the US operate on 110–120 volts and use two-prong plugs. Non-US, single-voltage appliances need a transformer and an adapter, commonly available in airport shops, electrical stores, and large department stores.

Driving Licenses

Foreign or out-of-state driver's licenses are valid in Chicago – if they are in English. Bring your picture license even if you don't plan to rent a car: it's a good alternative to a passport if you are asked for proof of age in a bar.

Weather

Chicago winters are usually intemperate, with frequent heavy snow and temperatures ranging from 13° F (-9° C) to 37° F (4° C). Summer days can be anything from balmy to boiling, averaging 69° F (22° C) to 84° F (30° C). Extremes, like winter blizzards, heavy spring rains, and summer heat waves are not uncommon, with spring-time weather being particularly changeable. Despite the winds that can gust off Lake Michigan, Chicago's "Windy City" moniker is actually attributed to the verbose bid the city made to host the 1893 World's Columbian Exposition.

When to Go

For a moderate climate, the best time to visit Chicago is spring or fall. But if you can bear the bitter cold of the festive season you'll see the city sparkle with Christmas lights – and you'll have a lot fewer tourists to contend with. Summer sees street festivities and live music in the parks. Try to avoid visiting in November, when hotels are full of conventioneers.

Travelers with Special Needs

The majority of hotels restaurants, shops, malls, and museums are accessible to wheelchair users. Many sidewalks offer curb cuts that allow smooth passage when crossing the streets. Most buses and train stations are also wheelchair accessible. The non-profit **Open Doors Organization** runs a website with information for travelers with disabilities. The **Mayor's Office for People with Disabilities** offers information on disabled access around town.

Sources of Information

Chicago has two main tourist information centers: located in the Chicago Cultural Center (see p71) and in Macy's department store (see p76) in the Loop. Opening hours are at least 10am–5pm Monday to Saturday and 11am–4pm Sunday (the Macy's location keeps department store hours). You can also get further

DIRECTORY

POSTAL SERVICES

US Postal Service
W usps.com

NEWSPAPERS AND MAGAZINES

Chicago Magazine
W chicagomag.com

Chicago Sun-Times
W chicago.suntimes.com

Chicago Tribune
W chicagotribune.com

The Reader
W chicagoreader.com

Time Out Chicago
W timeout.com/chicago

TRAVELERS WITH SPECIAL NEEDS

Mayor's Office for People with Disabilities
W cityofchicago.org

Open Doors Organization
W easyaccesschicago.org

SOURCES OF INFORMATION

Choose Chicago
W choosechicago.com

Eater Chicago
W chicago.eater.com

MetroMix
W metromix.com

Theatre in Chicago
W theatreinchicago.com

information at the city's official tourism website **Choose Chicago**, which is updated regularly. For in-depth reviews of where to go and what to see, log onto **MetroMix**, affiliated to the *Chicago Tribune*. The popular web site **Eater Chicago** offers comprehensive dining information. **Theatre in Chicago**, also online, offers up-to-date information on shows around town.

Trips and Tours

Run by Choose Chicago, the free **Chicago Greeters** service gives you a chance to spend 2 to 4 hours with enthusiastic locals who love the city (book online 10 days in advance). For more spontaneous tours, **InstaGreeters** are available for hour-long tours Friday to Sunday.

For design buffs, the **Chicago Architectural Foundation** tours offer itineraries focused on the city's architecture by walking, bike, bus, or (in summer) boat tour. The trips highlight both historic and modern buildings, including Frank Lloyd Wright's architectural legacy. They also run occasional Loop Train Tours – a great opportunity to glimpse ornate facades that are often invisible from the sidewalks below.

Delve into some of the city's infamous 1920s and 1930s gangster residents with **Untouchable Tours**. On board a custom-built bus, sites visited on this 2-hour tour include that of the St. Valentine's Day Massacre, Little Italy.

Many boat companies, including **Wendella** and **Shoreline Sightseeing**, offer ways to see the city from the river and the lake. Leaving from Navy Pier, **Seadog Cruises** provide tours of both in fast speedboats. Enjoy a meal or cocktails and dancing onboard the elegant *Odyssey* or *Spirit of Chicago* mega-yachts, also moored at Navy Pier. In summer, their neighbor, the four-masted schooner *Windy*, also sails the lake.

More active options for exploring include tours from **Bike & Roll Chicago**. Cycling tours will guide you through the city's parks, neighborhoods, or along the lakefront. Themed departures include yoga and biking, brewery by bike, and food tours. The company also offers itineraries via Segways. **Bobby's Bike Hike** also offers themed cycling tours.

Paddle down the Chicago River while learning about the city's history with **Wateriders**; they offer gangster- and ghost-themed tours for both beginners and advanced paddlers.

Shopping

Chicago is a great shopping destination, combining all the major brands and designers with neighborhood boutiques and interesting art and craft galleries.

You're in shopper's heaven when it comes to department stores, which are mostly located on North Michigan Avenue and State Street. They include traditional **Macy's**, upscale **Nordstrom**, and stylish **Bloomingdale's**.

There's no shortage of malls in the city, especially vertical ones on the Mag Mile. Here you'll find **Water Tower Place**, **Westfield North Bridge**, and **900 North Michigan Shops**. Among discount stores, look for bargains at **Nordstrom Rack** in two downtown locations.

Authentic local food, such as pizza and Eli's cheesecake, can be shipped anywhere in the US by **Taste of Chicago**.

Many Chicago stores have items on sale all year round, but expect real bargains after Christmas, on Presidents' Day (third Monday in February), and on Labor Day (first Monday in September).

Chicago state and local sales taxes are among the highest in the country at 10.25 percent on all non-food items.

Clothing and shoe sizes in the UK, Europe, and the US differ. Look at www.onlineconversion.com for help with sizes.

Where to Eat

Chicago is considered one of the country's dining meccas, with specialties at both the high and low ends of the scale, including acclaimed chef-run restaurants and beefy steakhouses down to popular hot dog and taco stands. The city is best known for its deep-dish pizza, which is highly filling, caloric, and fun.

Restaurant styles run the gamut from gourmet to casual, and many neighborhoods are hives of ethnic cuisine. Most chef-run places will accommodate dietary restrictions, and many restaurants label dishes if they are vegan, vegetarian, low-calorie or gluten-free.

Most restaurants take reservations and many require advance booking on weekends. The free restaurant reservation site **Open Table** is a good source for one-click tables.

With the exception of very high-end places, most restaurants are family friendly, offering kids' menus, high chairs, and even crayons.

This is especially true at neighborhood restaurants, though hotel eateries are also very accommodating.

Breakfast is usually served in diners and coffee shops from about 6am to 10am. Lunch is normally available from 11:30am to 2pm, and dinner takes place from approximately 5 to 10pm, depending on the spot.

Tipping is expected for waiters at 15–20 percent of the bill before taxes. Taxes will add 10.7 percent to your food bill.

Where to Stay

Chicago offers every kind of accommodation possible, from a berth on a boat to a luxury hotel. The former and other unusual options, as well as a room in someone's home, can be found at **Airbnb**. The popular home-sharing service can often source entire apartments at bargain rates.

Most accommodations are in hotels, which vary from big convention-focused options to small and stylish boutiques. The best in terms of location are downtown.

Hotel rates vary according to the hotel category, and the time of week and season. Peak rates are from April to December and often coincide with business travel traffic in town. This means weekends can be a good time to save, though summer rates are highest no matter what day of the week. Rack rates (the basic room rates) are the ones used in this book to provide a guide price. It is almost always possible to get a better deal, so don't be too shy to ask. Usually, the larger the room, the higher the tab, and many, though not all, hotels charge more for a room with a view – so consider how much time you will want to spend in your room before you pay the premium. Twin-bedded rooms are uncommon; most double rooms have either a queen- or king-sized bed or two double beds. Rates are subject to a 17.4 percent hotel tax. For hotel deals, see **Hotel Tonight** or **Booking.com.**

The selection of B&Bs, listed at the **Chicago Bed and Breakfast Association (CBBA)**, are a great way to see the city from a new perspective.

DIRECTORY

TRIPS AND TOURS

Bike & Roll Chicago
w bikechicago.com

Bobby's Bike Hike
w bobbysbikehike.com

Chicago Architectural Foundation
w architecture.org

Chicago Greeters and InstaGreeters
w chicagogreeter.com

Odyssey
w odysseycruises.com

Seadog Cruises
w seadogcruises.com

Shoreline Sightseeing
w shorelinesightseeing.com

Spirit of Chicago
w spiritcruises.com

Untouchable Tours
w gangstertour.com

Wateriders
w wateriders.com

Wendella
w wendellaboats.com

Windy
w tallshipwindy.com

SHOPPING

900 North Michigan Shops
MAP L2 ■ 900 N. Michigan Ave.
w shop900.com

Bloomingdale's
MAP L2 ■ 900 N. Michigan Ave.
w bloomingdales.com

Macy's
MAP K4 ■ 111 N. State St.
w macys.com

Nordstrom
MAP L3 ■ 520 N. Michigan Ave.
w nordstrom.com

Nordstrom Rack
MAP K4 ■ 24 N. State St. and 101 E. Chicago Ave.
w nordstromrack.com

Tastes of Chicago
w tastesofchicago.com

Water Tower Place
MAP L2 ■ 835 N. Michigan Ave.
w shopwatertower.com

Westfield North Bridge
MAP L3 ■ 520 N. Michigan Ave.
w theshopsatnorthbridge.com

WHERE TO EAT

Open Table
w opentable.com

WHERE TO STAY

Airbnb
w airbnb.com

Booking.com
w booking.com

CBBA
w chicago-bed-breakfast.com

Hotel Tonight
w hoteltonight.com

Places to Stay

PRICE CATEGORIES

For a standard, double room per night (with breakfast if included), taxes and extra charges.

....

$ under $200 $$ $200–$400 $$$ over $400

Luxury Hotels

The Gwen

MAP L3 ▪ 521 N. Rush St. ▪ 312-645-1500 ▪ www. thegwenchicago.com ▪ $$

Tucked discreetly above the Shops at North Bridge on the Magnificent Mile, the 300-room Gwen, lodged in the historic 1929 McGraw-Hill Building, takes its name from sculptress Gwen Lux whose relief panels adorn the hotel. Its fifth-floor terrace bar is a haven on the teeming street.

InterContinental Chicago

MAP L2 ▪ 505 N. Michigan Ave. ▪ 312-944-4100 ▪ www.icchicago. com ▪ $$

This former men's club (see p32) has stunning public rooms, including a swimming pool, and very comfortable guest rooms. The mix of historic charm with contemporary elegance makes it one of the city's most luxurious hotels

Trump International Hotel & Tower

MAP K3 ▪ 401 N. Wabash Ave. ▪ 312-588-8000 ▪ www.trumpchicago hotel.com ▪ $$

Chicago's second-highest building (at 92 stories) houses this chic and state-of-the-art hotel. Stylish rooms have electronic amenities and floor-to-ceiling windows with views of Lake Michigan, the Chicago River, and the city skyline.

Four Seasons

MAP L2 ▪ 120 E. Delaware Pl. ▪ 312-280-8800 ▪ www.fourseasons.com ▪ $$$

One can expect the best in this grand hotel – possibly Chicago's most elegant. Lavish rooms command sweeping city and lake views, and the award-winning Seasons restaurant is a must-try.

Langham Chicago

MAP K3 ▪ 330 N. Wabash Ave. ▪ 312-923-9988 ▪ www.langhamhotels. com ▪ $$$

This branch of the Hong Kong-based luxury hotel bridges worldly splendor and mid-century modern Chicago, a cue it takes from its location in a Mies van der Rohe-designed high-rise. The popular second-story bar looks out over the Chicago River and the Chuan Spa offers unusual Asian treatments.

Park Hyatt Chicago

MAP L2 ▪ 800 N. Michigan Ave. ▪ 312-335-1234 ▪ www.parkchicago. hyatt.com ▪ $$$

Original contemporary art, rich woods, and warm tones create comfortable and tranquil public and private areas at this elegant boutique hotel. The state-of-the-art

rooms and suites feature furniture designed by Mies van der Rohe. Other facilities include an indoor pool and fitness center.

Peninsula Chicago

MAP L2 ▪ 108 E. Superior St. ▪ 312-337-2888 ▪ www.peninsula.com/ chicago ▪ $$$

Understated elegance sums up this hotel, with large, earth-toned rooms that include dressing areas, and a steam-free TV screen and hands-free telephone in every bathroom. Floor-to-ceiling windows dramatize the lobby, where afternoon tea is accompanied by live classical music.

Ritz-Carlton

MAP L2 ▪ 160 E. Pearson St. ▪ 312-266-1000 ▪ www.fourseasons.com ▪ $$$

The Ritz has it all – first-class service, an award-winning dining room, spa, and the best business facilities. Great views complement the classic furniture and fine art in its spacious guest rooms, but it's the little things, like Bulgari toiletries and toys and cookies for the kids, that puts it in a league of its own.

Sofitel Chicago Water Tower

MAP K2 ▪ 20 E. Chestnut St. ▪ 312-324-4000 ▪ www.sofitel.com ▪ $$$

This striking, ultra-modern hotel features spectacular views, sumptuous feather beds, and marble bathrooms in every room. There is also a 24-hour fitness center.

Historic Hotels

Palmer House Hilton
MAP L4 ▪ 17 E. Monroe St. ▪ 312-726-7500 ▪ www.chicagohilton.com ▪ $
This has been an elegant fixture in the heart of the Loop since 1873. Extravagant frescoes decorate the ornate lobby's ceiling, while the guest rooms are subtly elegant. The hotel has its own shopping arcade.

The Tremont
MAP K2 ▪ 100 E. Chestnut St. ▪ 312-751-1900 ▪ www.tremontchicago.com ▪ $
An inviting fireplace welcomes you at this 1920s-built hotel, where guest rooms are small but comfortable; some have antique furniture and four-posters. Mike Ditka's restaurant is famous for its steaks and sports memorabilia.

Chicago Athletic Association
MAP L4 ▪ 12 S. Michigan Ave. ▪ 312-940-3552 ▪ www.chicagoathletichotel.com ▪ $$
Originally opened in 1893 as a men's club, the reincarnation of this building as a hotel faithfully restored all the terrazzo floors, stained glass, marble staircases, and other adornments. The rooftop restaurant and the vintage-game-filled bar are among the highlights.

Millennium Knickerbocker
MAP L2 ▪ 163 E. Walton Pl. ▪ 312-751-8100 ▪ www.millenniumhotels.com ▪ $$
This hotel, once owned by Playboy magazine, has hosted guests as famous as John Kennedy and Al Capone. Its 1930s lobby holds the Martini Bar (with live music most days), and the guest rooms exude a timeless elegance.

The Talbott
MAP K2 ▪ 20 E. Delaware Pl. ▪ 312-944-4970 ▪ www.talbotthotel.com ▪ $$
Enjoy the quiet elegance of this small, family-owned, European-style hotel. The Victorian parlor-like lobby and atmospheric Basil's bar and café offer a chance to unwind, and the 149 guest rooms and suites are large and welcoming.

Wheeler Mansion
2020 S. Calumet Ave. ▪ 312-945-2020 ▪ www.wheelermansion.com ▪ $$
An immaculate 11-room hotel, this mansion dating to 1870 is known for its fantastic attention to detail. Marvel at the lavish artwork, period features, and antique furniture, or relax in the tranquil garden.

The Whitehall
MAP L2 ▪ 105 E. Delaware Pl. ▪ 312-944-6300 ▪ www.thewhitehallhotel.com ▪ $$
A quiet, understated European ambience has permeated this hotel since it opened in 1928. The 221 guest rooms combine elegant tradition with mod cons, and the Presidential Suite was a favorite of Katharine Hepburn. Check out the Fornetto Mei restaurant with its menu of neo-Milanese cuisine and thin-crust specialty pizzas.

The Drake
MAP L2 ▪ 140 E. Walton Pl. ▪ 312-787-2200 ▪ www.thedrakehotel.com ▪ $$$
Popular with visiting celebrities and royalty, this is the *grande dame* of Chicago hotels. A landmark building on the Magnificent Mile, The Drake effortlessly blends modern convenience with the charm of days gone by. Each of the 535 rooms and suites is unique, and many of them offer breathtaking views.

Hotel Burnham
MAP K4 ▪ 1 W. Washington St. ▪ 312-782-1111 ▪ www.burnhamhotel.com ▪ $$$
The Reliance Building *(see p42)* – a handsome example of the Chicago school of architecture – was reborn as the boutique Hotel Burnham in 1999. Plush rooms are decorated in gold and blue, some with great views. A complimentary wine reception is held every evening.

Designer Hotels

Dana Hotel & Spa
MAP K2 ▪ 660 N. State St. ▪ 312-202-6000 ▪ www.danahotelandspa.com ▪ $
Chic and contemporary, this boutique hotel features rooms with modern furnishings, floor-to-ceiling windows, Wi-Fi, a state-of-the-art sound system, fine linens, and a double-sized shower. Guests can enjoy a range of services available at the spa, while the hotel restaurant, Ajasteak, provides a delectable range of Asian dishes.

The James
MAP L2 ▪ 55 E. Ontario St. ▪ 312-337-1000 ▪ www.jameshotels.com/chicago ▪ $
Modern and sleek, The James feels like a home away from home. Rooms have comfortable platform beds, a small dining area, plasma TVs, stereos with MP3 docks, free Wi-Fi, and marble bathrooms.

Godfrey Hotel Chicago
MAP K2 ▪ 127 W. Huron St. ▪ 312-649-2000 ▪ www.godfreyhotelchicago.com ▪ $$
Housed in a new high-rise in trendy River North, the Godfrey offers considerable social appeal via its rooftop lounge, partially glassed-in for four-season service, with a video wall and fire pit. Its 221 rooms are loft-like and amenities include a spa and Italian restaurant.

Hard Rock Hotel
MAP L2 ▪ 230 N. Michigan Ave. ▪ 312-345-1000 ▪ www.hardrockhotelchicago.com ▪ $$
This extravagant 381-room, musically themed hotel occupies the Carbide and Carbon building – an Art Deco creation of 1929. Piped music and memorabilia are everywhere, and rooms are stylish but fun.

Hotel Allegro
MAP J4 ▪ 171 W. Randolph St. ▪ 312-236-0123 ▪ www.allegrochicago.com ▪ $$
Designer Cheryl Rowley has combined classic Art Deco features with contemporary colors and textures to great effect at this vibrant,

musically themed hotel. Complimentary wine is offered nightly to guests.

Radisson Blu Aqua Hotel Chicago
MAP L3 ▪ 221 N. Columbus Dr. ▪ 312-565-5258 ▪ www.radissonblu.com ▪ $$
In the undulating Aqua Tower, the 334-room Radisson Blu Aqua gives guests access to extensive amenities, including indoor and outdoor pools. The hotel's useful app offers a tour of its extensive art collection.

Soho House Chicago
MAP H4 ▪ 113 N. Green St. ▪ 312-521-8000 ▪ www.sohohouse chicago.com ▪ $$
Belonging to the stylish Soho House clubs, the Chicago branch occupies a 19th-century factory marrying refined and raw materials, such as exposed brick walls and chandeliers. Guests have access to a members-only rooftop bar and pool, private lounge, and gym.

Thompson Chicago
MAP K1 ▪ 21 E. Bellevue Pl. ▪ 312-266-2100 ▪ www.thompsonhotels.com ▪ $$
In a good location in the Gold Coast area, the 247-room Thompson Chicago manages to make this bland high-rise engaging, through organic materials and intriguing art. Window-walled rooms, the higher the better, offer skyline views. One of Chicago's best chefs, Paul Kahan, runs the excellent Nico Osteria here, as well as the cocktail bar in the convivial lobby.

Virgin Hotels Chicago
MAP L3 ▪ 203 N. Wabash Ave. ▪ 312-940-4400 ▪ www.virginhotels.com ▪ $$
Sir Richard Branson has reinvented this hotel with good design and humor. Rooms feature sliding doors between the foyer and bedroom and ceramic dogs indicate pet-friendly rooms. Eat and drink in the first-floor diner or rooftop bar.

W Chicago Lakeshore
MAP M3 ▪ 644 N. Lake Shore Dr. ▪ 312-943-9200 ▪ www.wchicago-lakeshore.com ▪ $$
A Zen water wall and "Leave me alone," rather than "Do not disturb" signs are indications of the W's hip take on the hotel experience.

Business Hotels

Courtyard by Marriott Chicago Downtown
MAP K3 ▪ 30 E. Hubbard St. ▪ 312-329-2500 ▪ www.courtyard.com ▪ $
Bright, modern rooms with high-speed Internet access, a spacious work area, and an extra sofa-bed make this centrally located hotel a popular choice among leisure and business travelers alike.

Hyatt Regency McCormick Place
MAP D5 ▪ 2233 S. Martin Luther King Jr. Dr. ▪ 312-567-1234 ▪ www.mccormickplace.hyatt.com ▪ $
Linked by a connecting walkway to McCormick Place convention center, the basic but modern rooms of the 32-story Hyatt Regency are an

attractive stopover for conventioneers. The hotel also has a fitness facility.

Residence Inn Chicago Downtown
MAP K4 ▪ 11 S. LaSalle St. ▪ 312-223-8500 ▪ www.marriott.com ▪ $
In a historic building in downtown the Loop, this extended-stay hotel offers more style than most in the category. Rooms are spacious and come with kitchens. Amenities include a fitness center and free Wi-Fi.

Embassy Suites Hotel O'Hare-Rosemont
5500 N. River Rd., Rosemont ▪ 1-847-678-4000 ▪ www.embassy ohare.com ▪ $$
This hotel's seven-story garden atrium makes a pleasant retreat from the hustle and bustle. Suites have all the necessary facilities; cooked breakfasts and an airport shuttle are complimentary.

Hyatt Regency Chicago
MAP L3 ▪ 151 E. Wacker Dr. ▪ 312-565-1234 ▪ www.chicagoregency.hyatt.com ▪ $$
A lobby full of greenery and fountains welcomes guests into this large hotel. Although all guest rooms offer high-speed Internet access, you can opt for a "Business Plan" upgrade to obtain more specific benefits.

Sheraton Chicago Hotel & Towers
301 E. North Water St. ▪ 312-464-1000 ▪ www.sheraton chicago.com ▪ $$
The large, stylish guest rooms here offer fantastic

lake, city, or river views. The hotel has a business center, boat dock, health club, and five restaurants.

Swissôtel
MAP L3 ▪ 323 E. Wacker Dr. ▪ 312-565-0565 ▪ www.swissotel.com ▪ $$
Rising up where the Chicago River and Lake Michigan meet is this dramatic glass-and-steel creation. Oversized rooms contain every convenience for the business traveler and provide stellar views across the city skyline.

Westin Chicago River North
MAP K3 ▪ 320 N. Dearborn St. ▪ 312-744-1900 ▪ www.westinchicago.com ▪ $$
This sleek, four-star venue is home to a state-of-the-art Executive Business Center, fitness facility, and guest rooms featuring the comfortable Westin Heavenly Bed.

Budget Accommodation

AC Hotel Chicago
MAP L2 ▪ 630 N. Rush St. ▪ 312-981-6600 ▪ www.marriott.com ▪ $
Neutral rooms are calm, cool, and refined in this Gold Coast hotel. The lounge offers a pleasant space to start or end your evening, the restaurant serves breakfast only, and the fitness facilities include an indoor pool.

Best Western River North
MAP K3 ▪ 125 W. Ohio St. ▪ 312-467-0800 or 1-800-727-0800 ▪ www.river northhotel.com ▪ $
The location of this hotel, a little east of

the Magnificent Mile, is excellent. Rooms are spacious, with free high-speed Internet access, in-room movies, and 30 minutes of local calls. There are also parking, fitness rooms, and an indoor pool.

Freehand Chicago
MAP L3 ▪ 19 E Ohio St. ▪ 312-940-3699 ▪ www.thefreehand.com ▪ $
The stylish Freehand bills itself as a hostel, and offers shared rooms, but it also acts as a budget hotel and has small private rooms with their own bathrooms. Furthermore, its chic cocktail lounge and restaurant attract locals as well as travelers.

Hampton Inn Chicago Downtown
MAP K3 ▪ 33 W. Illinois St. ▪ 312-832-0330 ▪ www.hamptonsuiteschicago.com ▪ $
Located in River North, the Hampton Inn offers good value just a block from the Magnificent Mile. Amenities include an indoor pool, fitness center, outdoor patio, free breakfast, and complimentary Wi-Fi. The on-site restaurant Joe Fish features Italian food.

Hostelling International Chicago
MAP L5 ▪ 24 E. Congress Pkwy. ▪ 312-360-0300 ▪ www.hichicago.org ▪ $
This place is great value if you don't mind sleeping in a basic dormitory with local students. You don't need to be a member in order to stay here. The facilities include lounges, fully equipped kitchens, and bed linen.

For a key to hotel price categories see p116

Index

Page numbers in **bold** refer to main entries.

860–80 N. Lake Shore Drive 42

A

A League of Their Own (film) 48
A Sunday on La Grande Jatte (Seurat) 15, 49
Accommodation 115
  hostelling 119
  see also Hotels
Achatz, Grant 61
Acrobats at the Cirque Fernando (Renoir) 14
Addams, Jane 41, 45, 97
Adler Planetarium 96
Adler and Sullivan 42
Air travel 108, 109
Airbnb 115
America Windows (Chagall) 15
American Gothic (Wood) 14
Amtrak trains 108, 109
Andersonville 62
Aqua Tower 43
Aquariums
  John G. Shedd Aquarium 11, **28–29**, 53, 95
Architects 43
Architectural Artifacts 63, 90
Architecture
  The Loop 74
Arlington Park 67
Armitage Avenue 63
Armitage/Halsted Shopping District 88
Art galleries see Museums and galleries
Art Institute of Chicago 10, **14–17**, 49
Arthur Heurtley House 37
Astor Street District 80
At the Moulin Rouge (Toulouse-Lautrec) 15
Atget, Eugène 17
ATMs 111
Auditorium Theatre 42
Aykroyd, Dan 48, 89

B

Baha'i Temple 50
Banking 111
  opening hours 112
Barber, Patricia 57

Bars 58–59, 91, 92, 98
Baseball
  Chicago Black Sox Scandal (1919) 40
  Chicago Cubs 67, 87
  Chicago White Sox 40, 67
  film locations 48
  Wrigley Field 48, 52, 86, 87
Basketball
  Chicago Bulls 67
Bayless, Rick 61
Beaches **46–47**
  Montrose Beach 46–47
  North Avenue Beach 46, 89
  Oak Street Beach 46
Beachy House 36
"The Bean" (sculpture) 34, 72
Belushi, John 48, 89
Bernard A. Mitchell Hospital 110, 111
Bicycling 109
  Divvy bikes 64, 65, 109
  rental bicycles 64
  tours 114, 115
Bird, Andrew 58
Bloomingdale's Home and Furniture Store 62
Blue Chicago 57
Blues Heaven Foundation 95
Blues joints 56–57
The Blues Brothers (film) 48
Boat tours 53, 114, 115
The Bootleg Houses 37
Botington, William W. 80
Boystown 87
BP Bridge 35
Brewery Tours 65
Broadway Antique Market 62
Broderick, Matthew 49
Bronzeville 51
Brookfield Zoo 50
Buckingham Fountain 73
Bucktown Neighborhood 62
Bullock, Sandra 49
Burnham, Daniel H. 43, 74, 96
Burroughs, Edgar Rice 36
Buses 108, 109

C

Calder, Alexander 64
  Flamingo 74
Capone, Al 40, 41, 49
Cars
  city travel 109
  driving licenses 113
  rental 108, 109
  rental insurance 110
Carson Pirie Scott Building 74
Cassatt, Mary
  The Child's Bath 15
Cellphones 112
Ceres (statue) 71
Chagall, Marc 49, 64
  America Windows 15
Chain Reaction (film) 48
Charles Matthews House 36
Charnley House 80
Checker Taxis 109
Cheney, Mamah 37
Chicago Air and Water Show 66
Chicago Architecture Foundation 6, 74, 79, 114
  CAF Shop 63
Chicago Bears 67
Chicago Bed and Breakfast Association (CBBA) 115
Chicago Black Sox Scandal (1919) 40
Chicago Blackhawks 67
Chicago Blues Festival 64, 66
Chicago Board of Trade 71
Chicago Botanic Garden 50
Chicago Bulls 67
Chicago Children's Museum 24, 52
Chicago Cubs 67, 87
Chicago Cultural Centre 65, 71, 84–85, 113
Chicago Dental Society 110, 111
Chicago Fire 67
Chicago Gospel Music Festival 66
Chicago Greeter tours 65, 114, 115
Chicago History Museum 87
Chicago Marathon 67
Chicago River 13, 40
  boat tours 53
Chicago (Sandburg) 34

Chicago Shakespeare
    Theater 25, 55
Chicago Symphony
    Orchestra 54, 75
Chicago Temple 75
Chicago Theatre 74
Chicago Theological
    Seminary 102, 104
Chicago Transit Authority
    (CTA) 108, 109
Chicago Triathlon 67
Chicago Tribune 80
Chicago Visitor Center 80
Chicago Water Taxi 109
Chicago Water Works and
    Pumping Station 34, 80
Chicago White Sox 40, 67
Chicago Wolves 67
Children
    Chicago Children's
        Museum 24, 52
    Kids' Chicago 52–53
The Child's Bath (Cassatt)
    15
Chinatown 94, 97
Choose Chicago 65, 113,
    114
Churches
    Chicago Temple 75
    Fourth Presbyterian
        Church 81
    Old St. Patrick's Church
        75
    Rockefeller Memorial
        Chapel 50
    Unity Temple 36
Cinema
    IMAX Theatre 24
    see also Film locations
CityPass 65
Civic Opera House 75
Clarke House 95
Climate 110, 113
Cloud Gate (Kapoor) 34, 72
Clubs 58–59, 98
Cobb, Henry Ives 81
Colbert, Stephen 89
Comedy shows 55, 64, 89
Concrete Traffic (Vostell)
    103
*Construction in Space in the
    Third and Fourth
    Dimension* (Pevsner) 103
Consulates 111
Costner, Kevin 49
Court Theatre 54
Courtesan (Dohan) 17
Cram, Ralph Adams 81
Credit cards 111
Crosby, Bing 82

Crown Fountains 34
Currency 111
Customs and immigration
    110
Cycling *see* Bicycling

D
Daley, Maggie 46
Daley Plaza 48, 75
DeNiro, Robert 49
Dental clinics 110
Dickens, Charles
    A Christmas Carol 55
Disabled travelers 113
Divvy bikes 64, 65, 109
Dixon, Willie 95
Dohan, Kaigetsudo
    Courtesan 17
The Drake Hotel 32, 48
Driving *see* Cars
Driving licenses 113
Drug stores 110
DuSable Museum of
    African American History
    44–45, 101
Duty-free allowance 110

E
Eater Chicago 113
Edwin Cheney House 37
Eggleston, William 96
Electrical appliances 113
Elite Chicago Limo 108,
    109
Elling, Kurt 57
Embassies 111
Emerald City Theatre
    Company 52
Emergency services 110
Entertainment
    free and discounted
        tickets 64, 65
Evanston 50
Exchange rates 111

F
Far South **100–105**
    area map 100
    exploring Far South 103
    restaurants 105
    shopping 104
Federal Center 74
Federal Reserve Bank 75
Fermi, Enrico 41
Ferris Bueller's Day Off
    (film) 48, 49
Festivals **66–67**
    free events 64
    neighbourhood festivals
        67

Fey, Tina 55, 89
Field Museum 10, **18–19**,
    48, 63, 94
Film locations 48–49
    see also Cinema
Fire services 110
Fisher, L.G. 74
Fisher Building 74
Flamingo (Calder) 74
Flash Cab Co. 109
Food and drink
    Brewery Tours 65
    festivals 67
    see also Restaurants
Foodseum Chicago 75
Football 67
Ford, Harrison 49
Fountain of Time (Taft) 103
Four Days in Chicago 6–7
Fourth Presbyterian
    Church 81
Frears, Stephen 48
Free Events and Tours
    64–65
The Fugitive (film) 49

G
Galleries *see* Museums
    and galleries
Gang, Jeanne 43
Garcia, Andy 48
Gardens *see* Parks and
    gardens
Garfield Park Conservatory
    51
Gates, Theaster, Jr 101
Gay community 87, 91
Gehry, Frank 34, 35, 73
Glessner House 95
GO Airport Express 108,
    109
Gold Coast Area 80
Goldberg, Bertrand 43
Goodman, Benny 41
Goodman Theatre 55, 73
Grant Park 13, 41, 46, 73
Great Chicago Fire (1871)
    33, 40, 72, 80, 81, 87
Green, Al 66
Greyhound buses 108,
    109
Griffin, Walter Burley 43
Grosse Point Lighthouse
    50
Guy, Buddy 57, 98

H
Hammond, Beeby, and
    Babka 72
Hanks, Tom 49

Harding Collection of Arms and Armor 17
Hargrove, Roy 66
Harold Washington Library Center 72
Harris Theater 34
Harry Adams House 37
Haymarket Riot (1886) 40
Health services 110, 111
Hefner, Hugh 41
Hellenic Museum and Cultural Center 44
Hemingway, Ernest 41, 51
Hero (film) 48
The Herring Net (Homer) 15
History **40–41**
Hockey 67
Holabird and Roche 74
Holabird and Root 71
Holabird, William 43
Holidays, public 112
Homer, Winslow
  The Herring Net 15
Hopper, Edward
  Nighthawks 14
Horse racing 67
Hospitals 110, 111
Hostelling International Chicago 111
Hotel Intercontinental 32
Hotels 115–119
  booking 115
  budget hotels 118
  business hotels 118–119
  designer hotels 117–118
  historic hotels 117
  luxury hotels 116
  prices 115
House Theatre 55
Hull House 41, 45, 97

I

Ice hockey 67
Ice-Skating Rink 35
Illinois Institute of Technology (IIT) 51
Impressionists 14, 15, 16
Inland Steel Building 74
InstaGreeters 65, 114, 115
Insurance 110
International Museum of Surgical Science 45
Internet 112
iO Theater 64–65
Izard, Stephanie 60

J

Jackson Park 23, 44, 46, 100
Jahn, Helmut 71

Jane Addams Hull House 41, 45, 97
Jay Pritzker Pavilion 34
Jazz 56–57, 66
Jenney, William Le Baron 40, 43
John G. Shedd Aquarium 11, **28–29**, 53, 95
John Hancock Center 12, 32, 42, 65, 74, 79
Jones, Tommy Lee 49
Jordan, Michael 13, 67, 87

K

Kahan, Paul 60
Kandinsky, Wassily 17
Kapoor, Anish
  Cloud Gate 34, 72, 73
Kennicott, John A. 102
Kenwood Historic District 102
Knuckles, Frankie 101
Kroc, Ray 41

L

"L" ("Elevated" trains) 52, 72–73, 108, 109
  Brown line 65
  first elevated train 40
  Randolph 49
Lagunitas Brewing 65
Lake Michigan 13
Lakefront Recreational Path 64
Lawrence, Robert 101
Legends of the Yuzu Nembutsu Sect (scroll painting) 17
Lesbian community
  Northside bars 91
Levy, Julien 17
Libraries
  Harold Washington Library Center 72
  Newberry Library 81
Lincoln, Abraham 87
Lincoln Park 47
Lincoln Park Conservatory 88
Lincoln Park Zoo 11, **30–31**, 53, 64, 88
Lollapalooza 66
Lookingglass Theatre 55, 80
The Loop **70–77**
  A Day in The Loop 73
  architectural sites 74
  area map 70–71
  Loop Sculpture Guide 64
  restaurants 77
  shopping 76

Lurie Garden 34
Lyric Opera of Chicago 54, 65, 75

M

McCormick Place 13
McCormick, Robert 80
McCormick Tribune Bridgehouse and River Museum 32
McDonald, Dick and Mac 41
McDonald's 41
Macy's 76, 113
Magazines 112, 113
Maggie Daley Park 46, 52, 75
Magnificent Mile 6, 11, **32–33**, 63, 78, 79
  Magnificent Mile Holiday Lights Festival 67
  map 33
Maher, George 36, 43
Malkovich, John 88
Mangiullo, Rosa and Tony 56
Mantuano, Tony 60
Maps
  A Day in the Near North 81
  A Day in The Loop 73
  bars and clubs 58
  Blues and Jazz Joints 56
  Chicago Highlights 10–11
  exploring Far South 103
  exploring Northside 89
  exploring South Loop 97
  Far South 100
  film locations 48
  Four Days in Chicago 7
  Kids' Chicago 52
  Lincoln Park Zoo 31
  The Loop 70–71
  Magnificent Mile 33
  Millennium Park 35
  Near North 78
  niche museums 44
  Northside 86
  Oak Park 37
  Off the Beaten Path 50
  parks and beaches 47
  performing arts 55
  restaurants 61
  South Loop 94–95
  Two Days in Chicago 7
Marina City 12, 42, 43
Markets 62, 96
Marquette Building 74
Marsalis, Branford 66
Mary & Leigh Block Museum of Art 45, 50

Matisse, Henri 17
Maxwell Street Market 96
Mayfield, Curtis 41
Mayor's Office for People
  with Disabilities 113
Medical services 110, 111
Megabus 108, 109
Merchandise Mart 13, 79
Merges, Mathias 59, 93
Metra trains 108, 109
MetroMix 113
Michigan Avenue Bridge
  32, 48
Midway International
  Airport 108, 109
Midway Plaisance 23, 100
Mies van der Rohe, Ludwig
  42, 43, 51
Millennium Monument
  35
Millennium Park 11,
  34–35, 46, 65
Miller, Penelope Ann 48
Mitchell, Joni 55
Mobile Phones 112
Monadnock Building 43, 74
Monet, Claude
  Stacks of Wheat 14
Montrose Beach 46–47
Monuments
  Millennium 35
  Pullman National
    Monument 51
Moore, Colleen 20
Moore, Henry
  Nuclear Energy 103
Moran, George ("Bugs")
  40–41
Murray, Bill 55, 89
Museums and galleries
  free museums 65
  niche museums 44–45
  opening hours 112
  Art Institute of Chicago
    10, **14–17**, 49
  Chicago Children's
    Museum 24, 52
  Chicago History Museum
    87
  DuSable Museum of
    African American History
    44–45, 101
  Field Museum 10, **18–19**,
    48, 63, 94
  Foodseum Chicago 75
  Hellenic Museum and
    Cultural Center 44
  Hull House 41, 45, 97
  International Museum of
    Surgical Science 45

Museums and galleries
  (cont.)
  McCormick Tribune
    Bridgehouse and River
    Museum 32
  Mary & Leigh Block
    Museum of Art 45, 50
  Museum Campus 73, 94
  Museum of
    Contemporary Art 34, 79
  Museum of
    Contemporary
    Photography 96
  Museum of Science and
    Industry 6, 10, **20–23**, 46,
    53, 102
  National Museum of
    Mexican Art 44, 65
  Oriental Institute 45, 100,
    102
  Peggy Notebaert Nature
    Museum 87
  Richard H. Driehaus
    Gallery of Stained Glass
    25
  River North Gallery
    District 80
  Smart Museum of Art 50
  Spertus Museum 44
  Stony Island Arts Bank
    101
  Swedish American
    Museum 44
  Tobacco museum 76
  Ukrainian Institute of
    Modern Art 45
Music 54, 55, 56–57

N
Nathan Moore House 37
National Museum of
  Mexican Art 44, 65
The Natural (film) 48
Navy Pier 7, 11, 13, **24–25**,
  53, 64
Near North **78–83**
  A Day in the Near North
    81
  area map 78
  restaurants 83
  shopping 82
Newberry, Walter L. 81
Newberry Library 81
Newspapers 112, 113
Nichols Bridgeway 35
Nighthawks (Hopper) 14
North Avenue Beach 46, 89
Northerly Island 47, 96
Northside **86–93**
  area map 86

Northside (cont.)
  exploring Northside 89
  gay and lesbian bars 91
  neighbourhood bars 92
  restaurants 93
  shopping 90
Northwestern Memorial
  Hospital 110, 111
Nuclear Energy (Moore) 103

O
Oak Park 11, **36–37**, 41, 51
Oak Street 62
Oak Street Beach 46
Obama, Barack 41, 103
Odyssey 114
O'Hare International
  Airport 108, 109
O'Keeffe, Georgia 17
The Old Guitarist (Picasso)
  14
Old St. Patrick's Church 75
Old Town Art Fair 67
Olmsted, Frederick Law
  23, 46, 100
On Leong Tong Building 97
One North LaSalle 74
O'Neill, Eugene 55
Open Doors Organization
  113
Open Table 114, 115
Opera 54
Oriental Institute 45, 100,
  102
Osaka Japanese Gardens
  102

P
PACE buses 108, 109
Palmer, Bertha Honoré 16
Palmer House Hilton 49,
  75
Parks and gardens **46–47**
  Chicago Botanic Garden
    50
  Garfield Park
    Conservatory 51
  Grant Park 13, 41, 46, 73
  Jackson Park 23, 44, 46,
    100
  Lincoln Park 47
  Maggie Daley Park 46,
    52, 75
  Millennium Park 11,
    34–35, 46, 65
  Northerly Island 47, 96
  Osaka Japanese
    Gardens 102
  Ping Tom Memorial Park
    47

Parks and gardens (cont.)
  Washington Park 103
  Washington Square 47
Passport requirements 110
Peggy Notebaert Nature
  Museum 87
Personal security 103, 109,
  111
Pevsner, Antoine
  *Construction in Space in
  the Third and Fourth
  Dimension* 103
Pharmacies 110
Piano, Renzo 14, 35, 73
Picasso, Pablo 17, 64
  The Old Guitarist 14
  "the Picasso" (sculpture)
  72, 75
Ping Tom Memorial Park 47
Planetarium
  Adler Planetarium 96
Playboy 41
Pleasant Home 36
Plensa, Jaume 34, 73
Poehler, Amy 55
Point du Sable, Jean
  Baptiste 41, 44–45,
  58–59, 101
Police 110
Postal services 112
Prairie architecture 36, 43
Prairie Avenue District
  94–95
Public holidays 112
Public phones 112
Pullman, George 51
Pullman National
  Monument 51

R
Radio 112
Randolph "L" Station 49
Reeves, Keanu 49
Reliance Building 42, 74
The Relic (film) 48
Renoir, Pierre-Auguste
  *Acrobats at the Cirque
  Fernando* 14
  Two Sisters 16
Rental cars 108, 109, 110
Restaurants 114–115
  Eater Chicago 113
  Far South 105
  The Loop 77
  money-saving tips 65
  Near North 83
  Northside 93
  reservations 114
  South Loop 99
  Top Ten 60–61

Revolution Brewing 65
Richard H. Driehaus
  Gallery of Stained Glass
  25
River North Gallery District
  80
Road to Perdition (film) 49
Robie House 102
Roche, Martin 43
  see also Holabird and
  Roche
Rockefeller, John D. 50
Rockefeller Memorial
  Chapel 50
Rookie of the Year (film) 48
The Rookery 42, 72
Rosenwald, Julius 23
Rubloff, Arthur 16
Ruck, Paul 49

S
Sandburg, Carl 41
  Chicago 34
Santa Fe Center 74
Sara, Mia 49
Saturday Night Live 89
Schwimmer, David 55
Sculpture 34, 72, 103
  Loop Sculpture Guide 64
Seadog Cruises 114, 115
Sears Roebuck and Co 42
Second City (comedy club)
  55, 89
Security 103, 109, 111
Seurat, Georges
  *A Sunday on La Grande
  Jatte* 15, 49
Shaw, Howard Van Doren
  102
Shedd, John G. 28
Shopping 114, 115
  Armitage/Halsted
  Shopping District 88, 89
  Far South 104
  malls 114
  Near North 82
  Northside 90
  opening hours 112
  souvenirs 63
  The Loop 76
  Top Ten Destinations
  62–63
Shoreline Sightseeing 114,
  115
Shoreline Water Taxis 109
Sinise, Gary 88
Sizemore, Tom 48
Skidmore, Owings &
  Merrill 42, 79
Skydeck 71

Skyscrapers 40, **42–43**
Smart Museum of Art 50
Soccer 67
Soldier Field 12
South Loop **94–99**
  area map 94–95
  bars and clubs 98
  restaurants 99
Souvenirs 63
Special needs travelers
  113
Spertus Museum 44
Sport
  Top Ten teams and
  events 67
  see also Baseball
Spirit of Chicago 114
Stacks of Wheat (Monet) 14
State Street 62
Steppenwolf Theatre
  Company 54, 86, 88
Stieglitz, Alfred 17
Stony Island Arts Bank
  101
Strand, Paul 17
Sugar Blue 56
Sullivan, Louis H. 37, 43,
  74, 80
  see also Adler and
  Sullivan
Swedish American
  Museum 44
Symphony Center 75

T
Taft, Lorado
  Fountain of Time 103
Tallmadge, Thomas Eddy
  36
Taste of Chicago 67, 114
Taxes
  hotel 115
  restaurants 115
  sales tax 114
Taxis 108, 109
Telephones 112
Television 112
Theater 54–55
  Auditorium Theatre
  42
  Chicago Shakespeare
  Theater 25, 55
  Chicago Theatre 74
  Court Theatre 54
  Emerald City Theatre
  Company 52
  Goodman Theatre
  55, 73
  half-price tickets
  65

Theater (cont.)
  Harris Theater 34
  House Theatre 55
  iO Theater 64–65
  Lookingglass Theatre 55, 80
  Loop Theater District 74
  Steppenwolf Theatre Company 54, 86, 88
  Theatre in Chicago 113
Theft 110
Thorne, Narcissa Ward 17
Tickets
  for public transport 109
Tiffany glass 25, 75, 84–85
Tiffany, Louis Comfort 25, 71
Time 112–113
Tipping
  restaurants 115
Tobacco museum 76
Toulouse-Lautrec, Henri de
  At the Moulin Rouge 15
Tourist information 113
Trains 108, 109
  to and from airport 108
  see also "L" ("Elevated" trains)
Travel **108–109**
  air 108, 109
  bicycling 64, 65, 109, 114, 115
  boat tours 53, 114, 115
  buses 108, 109
  cars 108, 109
  getting into the city 108
  safety 111
  taxis 108, 109
  tickets 109
  trains 108, 109
Travel insurance 110
Traveler's checks 111
Tribune Tower 34, 43, 63, 80

Two Days in Chicago 6
Two Sisters (Renoir) 16

U
Uber 109
Ukrainian Institute of Modern Art 45
Union Station 49, 108
United Center 13
Unity Temple 36
University of Chicago 50, 101, 103
  Oriental Institute 45, 100, 102
University of Illinois at Chicago 96
Untouchable Tours 114, 115
The Untouchables (film) 49
UP Comedy Club 89
US Customs and Border Protection 110, 111
US Department of Homeland Security 11, 110
US Postal Service 112

V
Valentine's Day Massacre (1929) 40–41
Vaux, Calvert 103
Visa requirements 110
Vostell, Wolf
  Concrete Traffic 103

W
Walgreens 110, 111
Washington, George 87
Washington, Harold 41, 72, 101
Washington Park 103
Washington Square 47
Water taxis 109
Water Tower Place 32, 63
Water Works Visitor Information Center 63

Wateriders 114, 115
Waters, Muddy 95
Watson, Vernon S. 36
Weather 110, 113
Weiss Memorial Hospital 110, 111
Wendella 114, 115
Weston, Edward 17
Wheelchair access 113
While You Were Sleeping (film) 49
White, Stanford 80
Wi-Fi 112
Willis Tower 7, 10, **12–13**, 71
Wilson, August 55
Windy 114
Winfrey, Oprah 41
Winogrand, Gary 96
Wood, Grant
  American Gothic 14
Wooded Island 102
World Music Festival 66–67
World's Columbian Exposition (1893) 23, 46, 87, 100
Wright, Frank Lloyd 36, 37, 43, 80, 102
  Art Institute of Chicago 17
  Oak Park 11, **36–37**
  Robie House 102, 103
Wrigley Building 34, 49
Wrigley Field 48, 52, 86, 87

Y
Yellow Cab Co. 109

Z
Zipcar 109
Zoos
  Brookfield Zoo 50
  Lincoln Park Zoo 11, **30–31**, 53, 88

Acknowledgments

Authors
Chicago-based freelancer Elaine Glusac specializes in travel writing for an array of publications including *National Geographic Traveler* and the *International Herald Tribune*.

Elisa Kronish ia a Chicago native who has written about the city's highlights and hidden finds for a varity of print and online travel guides such as Citysearch Chicago.

Roberta Sotonoff is a travel junkie. She writes about a variety of travel destinations, and her work has appeared worldwide in more than 40 newspapers, magazines, online sites, and guidebooks.

Publishing Director Georgina Dee

Publisher Vivien Antwi

Design Director Phil Ormerod

Editorial Michelle Crane, Rachel Fox, Sally Schafer, Jackie Staddon, Sophie Wright

Design Tessa Bindloss, Richard Czapnik, Stuti Tiwari Bhatia

Commissioned Photography Alessandra Santarelli and Joeff Davis, Andrew Leyerle, Rough Guides/Greg Roden, Jim Warych

Picture Research Susie Peachey, Ellen Root, Lucy Sienkowska, Oran Tarjan

Cartography Subhashree Bharti, Suresh Kumar, James Macdonald, Alok Pathak

DTP Jason Little, George Nimmo

Production Olivia Jeffries

Factchecker Lauren Viera

Proofreader Susanne Hillen

Indexer Rohan Bolton

Illustrator Lee Redmond

First edition created by Departure Lounge, London

Revisions Team
Rada Radojicic, Akshay Rana, Stuti Tiwari Bhatia

Picture Credits
The publisher would like to thank the following for their kind permission to reproduce their photographs:

Key: a-above; b-below/bottom; c-centre; f-far; l-left; r-right; t-top

123RF.com: Radomír Režný 26-7.

4Corners: SIME/Gabriele Croppi 2tl, 8-9.

Adler Planetarium: 96tl.

Alamy Stock Photo: A.F. Archive 41tr, 48tr, 49cra; age fotostock/Alan Copson 1b, /Steve Dunwell 82br; Felix Choo 24cla; Ian Dagnall 64b; Danita Delimont//Russell Gordon 29c, /Alan Klehr 102-3;

Craig M. Eisenberg 28cr; Richard Ellis 55c; Gino's Premium Images 10c; Glowimages RM 86tl; Kim Karpeles 36b, National Museum of Mexican Art 44crb, 46cl; Jason Lindsey 61tr; LOOK Die Bildagentur der Fotografen GmbH/Franz Marc Frei 59b; MARKA/Patrick Frilet 95tr; Cathyrose Melloan 16c; National Geographic Creative/Richard Nowitz 81cl; Nikreates 4b, 11bl, 37tr; North Wind Picture Archives 40tl; PF-(bygone1) 23cb; Philip Scalia/ *Unity Temple* by Frank Lloyd Wright © ARS, NY and DACS, London 2016 36-7; Pictorial Press Ltd 40crb; Scott B. Rosen 4cl; Henryk Sadura 23b; Helen Sessions 24br, /*Crown Fountains* by Jaume Plensa © DACS 2016 33cla, 82cl; Don Smetzer 87crb; Tribune Content Agency LLC/McClatchy 67tr; Michael Ventura 17tr; ZUMA Press, Inc. 48br.

Art Effect: 90c.

Photography © The Art Institute of Chicago: 16b; *The Child's Bath* 1893) by Mary Cassatt. Oil on canvas. 100.3 x 66.1 cm (39 1/2 x 26 in.) Robert A. Waller Fund 15bl; *Nighthawks* (1942) by Edward Hopper, Oil on canvas. 33 1/8 x 60 in. (84.1 x 152.4 cm). Friends of American Art Collection. 14cla; *Two Sisters (On the Terrace)* (1881) by Pierre Auguste Renoir. Oil on canvas. 39 9/16 x 37 7/8 in. (100.5 x 81 cm) Mr. and Mrs. Lewis Larned Coburn Memorial Collection 16tl; *At the Moulin Rouge* (1892/95) by Henri de Toulouse-Lautrec. Oil on canvas. 48 7/16 x 55 1/2 in. (123 x 141 cm) Helen Birch Bartlett Memorial Collection. 15t; *American Gothic* (1930) by Grant Wood. Friends of American Art Collection 14cb.

Buddy Guy's Legends: Anthony Moser 57tr;Aaron Porter 98b.

Chicago Shakespeare Theater: James Steinkamp 54b.

The Chicago Symphony Orchestra: Todd Rosenburg Photography 75b.

Choose Chicago: Adam Alexander Photography 4cra, 47br, 52tr, 57clb, 59cra, 65tr, 66tr, 70cla, 76t; City of Chicago 28cla, 88b, /Burnham & Root 72cl, /Patrick L. Pyszka 67cl, 84-5; Patrick L. Pyszka 66b, Brian Schilling 11clb.

Corbis: Arcaid/Jon Miller/Hedrich Blessing 54tl; imageBROKER/Uwe Kazmaier 32-3; Zuma Press/Nancy Stone 101br.

The Door: Eric Kleinberg 83c.

Dreamstime.com: Adeliepenguin 12-3; Americanspirit 12bl, 42br; Bambi L. Dingman 97cl; Thomas Barrat 50tl; Benkrut 36c; Blanscape 101t; Noah Browning 80tl; Bryan Busovicki 3tl, 68-9; Cafebeanz Company 88tr, 102cla; Cammelloribelle 80c; Clio85 34br; Cmlndm 6br, 94cra; Demerzel21 2tr, 38-9, 74clb; F11photo 35br, 46tl, 74tl; Alexandre Fagundes De Fagundes 33tl; Eugene Feygin 12cla; Cao Hai 11crb, 33bl; Jillian Cain 34-5; Kan1234 13br; Grzegorz Kieca 72bl Jessica Kirsh 73cl; Jesse Kraft 3tr, 106-7; Lightpainter 87t; Charlene C. Love 7cr; Maisna 65cl; Marchello74 4t; Mramos7637 32bl; Glenn Nagel 51cr, 62cl; Rhbabiak13 4cla; Michael Rosebrock 6cla;

Rudi1976 10cl, 71tr; Shutterfree Llc/R. Gino Santa Maria 4crb, 94cl; Sianamira 79b; Theresasc75 11cra, 96br; Tupungato 63cla; Vplut 35tl.

Courtesy of the **DuSable Museum of African-American History:** Dorling Kinderlsey Ltd/Santarelli Alessandra and Joeff Davis 45t.

Edible Ink PR: Stronghold Photography/Neil John Burger 91b.

Field Museum: 18cl, 18-9, 19cb; Greg Neise 10crb, 19tr, 19br.

Foodseum: 75cr.

Getty Images: Timothy Hiatt 64tl; Museum of Science and Industry Chicago 23tl; Scott Olson 63br; Helen H. Richardson 92tl; UniversalImagesGroup 43tl; The Washington Post/Brett T. Roseman 90tr.

Half Acre Beer Company: Beer Bokeh 92crb.

Hogsalt Hospitality: California Clipper 57br.

iStockphoto.com: stevegeer 24-5.

John G. Shedd Aquarium: Brenna Hernandez 53b.

Lincoln Park Zoo: 11cr, 30cla; Greg Neise 30-1, 31br; Todd Rosenberg Photography 30crb, 30br.

Museum of Science and Industry, Chicago, Il: 20-1, 21cr, 22tl, 53cr; J.B. Spector 10bl, 20cl, 20bl, 21tl.

Navy Pier, Inc: Nick Ulivieri 11tl.

North Pond Restaurant: 93cr.

One Off Hospitality Group, LTD: Jetel Fogelson 83tr; Chloe List 60bc.

The Promontory: 105r, Clayton Hauck 105clb.

Rex by Shutterstock: Courtesy Everett Collection 43br; KPA/Zuma 41bl; Paramount/Everett 49b; Universal Images Group/Universal History Archive 41tl.

The Richard H. Driehaus Museum: John Faier 4clb, 25bc.

Robert Harding Picture Library: Amanda Hall 79tr, 89cl; Henryk Sadura 48clb; Michael Weber 28-9.

Rosa's Lounge: 56tl.

Seminary Co-op Bookstore: Hedrich Blessing/ Steve Hall 104t.

Thomas Hart Shelby- Goat Rodeo Productions: 77cra.

Ukrainian Institute of Modern Art: 45c.

Wagstaff Worldwide: Galdones Photography/ Spiaggia Restaurant 60cr.

Willis Tower/FleishmanHillard: 7tl, 71br.

Cover
Front and spine: **Alamy Stock Photo:** Ian Dagnall.
Back: **Dreamstime.com:** Benkrut

Pull Out Map Cover
Alamy Stock Photo: Ian Dagnall.

All other images © Dorling Kindersley.
For further information see: www.dkimages.com

As a guide to abbreviations in visitor information blocks: **Adm** *= admission charge;* **DA** *= disabled access*

Penguin Random House

Printed and bound in China

First American Edition, 2004
Published in the United States by
DK Publishing, 345 Hudson Street,
New York, New York 10014

Copyright 2004, 2017 © Dorling
Kindersley Limited

A Penguin Random House Company

17 18 19 20 10 9 8 7 6 5 4 3 2 1

**Reprinted with revisions 2006, 2008,
2010, 2012, 2014, 2017**

Published in the UK by Dorling
Kindersley Limited

A catalog record for this book is available
from the Library of Congress.

ISSN 1479-344X
ISBN 978 1 4654 5735 6

MIX
Paper from
responsible sources
FSC™ C018179

SPECIAL EDITIONS OF DK TRAVEL GUIDES

DK Travel Guides can be purchased in bulk quantities at discounted prices for use in promotions or as premiums. We are also able to offer special editions and personalized jackets, corporate imprints, and excerpts from all of our books, tailored specifically to meet your own needs.

To find out more, please contact:

in the US
specialsales@dk.com

in the UK
travelguides@uk.dk.com

in Canada
specialmarkets@dk.com

in Australia
penguincorporatesales@
penguinrandomhouse.com.au

Selected Street Index

8th Street, East	K5	Cottage Grove Ave.,	
9th Street, East	K5	South	D6
11th Street, East	K6	Daley Plaza	K4
13th Street, East	K6	Damen Avenue	B4
18th Street, West	B5	Dan Ryan Expressway	H4
31st Street, East	A5	Dearborn Street, North	K3
47th Street, West	B6	Dearborn Street, South	K5
51st Street, East	D5	Delaware Place, East	K2
52nd Street, East	E5	Des Plaines Street,	
53rd Street, East	E5	South	J4
54th Street, East	E5	Devon Avenue	B3
55th Street, East	E5	Dickens Avenue, West	E3
56th Street, East	E5	Diversey Parkway, West	E2
57th Street, East	E6	Division Street, East	K1
58th Street, East	E6	Division Street, West	J1
59th Street, East	E6	Dorchester Avenue,	
60th Street, East	E6	South	E6
61st Street, East	E6	Drexel Boulevard,	
63rd Street, East	E6	South	E5
Ada Street, North	G3	Eisenhower	
Adams Street, West	J4	Expressway	A5
Addison Road, West	D1	Elizabeth Avenue,	
Archer Avenue	A6	North	G3
Armitage Avenue,		Ellis Avenue, South	E5
West	E4	Elm Street, East	L1
Ashland Avenue,		Elm Street, West	K1
North	D2	Erie Street, East	L2
Ashland Avenue,		Erie Street, West	K2
South	G5	Eugenie Street, West	F4
Aveland Avenue, West	D1	Fairbanks Court, North	L2
Balbo Avenue, East	L5	Franklin Street, North	J2
Barry Avenue, West	E2	Franklin Street, South	J5
Belden Avenue, West	E3	Fremont Street, North	E4
Bellevue Place, East	L1	Fullerton Avenue, West	D3
Belmont Avenue, West	E2	Fullerton Parkway,	
Blackstone Avenue,		West	E3
South	F5	Fulton Street, West	H3
Blue Island Avenue,		Garfield Boulevard	D5
South	H6	George Avenue, West	E2
Broadway	E2	Goethe Street, East	K1
Bryn Mawr Avenue	A3	Goethe Street, West	J1
Buckingham Road,		Grace Road, West	D1
West	E2	Grand Avenue, East	L3
Burling Avenue, North	E3	Grand Avenue, West	K3
Canal Street, North	J3	Greenwood Avenue,	
Canal Street, South	J5	South	E5
Cannon Drive, North	F3	Halsted Street, North	E2
Cedar Street, East	L1	Halsted Street, South	H6
Central Avenue	A4	Harper Avenue, South	F5
Cermak Road	B5	Harrison Street, East	K5
Chestnut Street, East	K2	Harrison Street, West	K5
Chestnut Street, West	K2	Hubbard Street, West	K3
Chicago Avenue, East	L2	Hudson Avenue, North	E4
Chicago Avenue, West	J2	Huron Street, East	L2
Cicero Avenue	A4	Huron Street, West	K2
Clark Street, North	E2	Hyde Park Boulevard,	
Cleveland Avenue,		South	F5
North	E3	Illinois Street, East	K3
Clifton Avenue, North	D2	Illinois Street, West	K3
Clinton Street, North	J4	Ingleside Avenue,	
Clinton Street, South	J4	South	E5
Clybourn Avenue,		Irving Park Road, West	D1
North	D3	Jackson Boulevard,	
Columbus Drive, North	L4	West	J4
Columbus Drive,		Jackson Drive, East	L4
South	L5	Jefferson Street, South	J4
Congress Parkway,		Kedzie Avenue	B4
West	K5	Kenmore Avenue,	
Congress Street, West	H5	North	E2
Cornell Avenue, South	F5	Kennedy Expressway	D4
Cornell Drive, South	F6		

Kenwood Avenue,		Randolph Street, East	L4
South	E6	Randolph Street, West	J4
Kimbark Avenue, South	E5	Roosevelt Road, East	L6
Kingsbury Street,		Roosevelt Road, West	J6
North	H1	Roscoe Road, West	E1
Kinzie Street, West	K3	Rush Street, North	L2
Lake Park Avenue,		Schiller Street, West	F4
South	F5	School Road, West	D2
Lake Shore Drive,		Scott Street, East	K1
South	L5	Scott Street, West	J1
Lake Street, East	L3	Sedgwick Street, North	J1
Lake Street, West	J3	Seminary Avenue,	
Lake View Avenue,		North	D2
North	E3	Sheffield Avenue,	
Lasalle Street, North	K2	North	E2
Lasalle Street, South	K5	Sheridan Road, North	E1
Lawrence Avenue	B3	Sheridan Road, West	E1
Lincoln Avenue, North	E3	Southport Avenue,	
Lincoln Park, North	F3	North	D1
Madison Street, East	K4	State Street, North	K2
Madison Street, West	J4	State Street, South	K6
Martin Luther King Jr.		Stetson Avenue, North	L3
Drive	D5	Stevenson Expressway	A6
Maxwell Street, West	J6	Stockton Drive, North	F3
Mcfetridge Drive	L6	Stony Island Avenue,	
Melrose Road, West	E2	South	F6
Michigan Avenue,		Superior Street, East	L2
North	L2	Superior Street, West	K2
Michigan Avenue,		Taylor Street, West	H6
South	L6	University Avenue,	
Milwaukee Avenue	B4	South	E5
Monroe Street, West	K4	Van Buren Street, East	K5
Montrose Avenue	A3	Van Buren Street, West	K5
Morgan Street, South	H5	Wabash Avenue,	
Newport Road, West	D1	North	K3
North Avenue, West	F4	Wabash Avenue,	
Oak Park Avenue	A5	South	K4
Oak Street, East	L1	Wacker Drive, East	L3
Oak Street, West	K1	Wacker Drive, South	J4
Oakdale Avenue, West	E2	Wacker Drive, West	K3
Ogden Avenue	B5	Walton Place, East	L2
Ohio Street, East	L3	Walton Street, West	K2
Ohio Street, West	K3	Washington Square	K2
Ontario Street, East	L2	Washington Street,	
Ontario Street, West	K2	West	J4
Orchard Avenue, North	E3	Webster Avenue, West	E3
Orleans Street, North	J2	Wellington Avenue,	
Pearson Street, East	L2	West	E2
Pershing Road	B6	Wells Street, North	K2
Peterson Avenue	A3	Wells Street, South	K5
Plaisance, North	E6	Western Avenue	B4
Plaisance, South	E6	Wisconsin Street, West	F4
Polk Street, West	K5	Woodlawn Avenue,	
Pulaski Road	A5	South	E5
Racine Avenue, North	G3	Wrightwood Avenue,	
Racine Avenue, South	G6	West	E3

Chicago's Grid System

Nearly all streets in Chicago run east–west or north–south. The zero point is at the intersection of Madison Street (running east–west) and State Street (running north–south). All streets are labelled in relation to this point: for example, the section of State Street north of Madison is known as North State Street. Numbering also begins at the zero point and odd numbers are on the east sides of north–south streets and the south sides of east–west streets.